THE BLENDER BOOK

THE
BLENDER
BOOK

Elm Tree Books in association with Hamish Hamilton Limited
for Thorn Domestic Appliances (Electrical) Limited

First published in Great Britain
by Elm Tree Books
in association with
Hamish Hamilton Limited
90 Great Russell Street London WC1

Part Copyright © 1967 by
Tested Recipe Publishers
This Volume Copyright © 1971
Elm Tree Books/Hamish Hamilton Ltd
First published in Great Britain 1971
Second Impression 1972
Third Impression December 1972
Fourth Impression April 1974

SBN 241 02078 6

Book layouts and decorations by
Norma Crockford

Photographs by
Paul Radkai

Accessories courtesy of
John Lewis and Harrods

Printed lithographically in Great Britain by
Ebenezer Baylis and Son Limited
The Trinity Press Worcester and London

CONTENTS

INTRODUCTION

'Cooking means carefulness, inventiveness, willingness and readiness of appliance. It means the economy of your grandmothers and the science of the modern chemist; it means much testing and no wasting; it means English thoroughness, French art, Arabian hospitality.'

These are Ruskin's words, as true and inspired today as they were when he wrote them eighty-five years ago.

For never before in the history of the culinary art has it been easier to prepare delectable food so economically and in such a minimum of time. Even in small households that do not run to the miracle of the omnipotent master chef, there are now small items of kitchen equipment designed for use in a dozen ways to make cooking more enjoyable and convenient.

One of these is the blender which caused a revolution when it was first introduced in America before the last war. In England it was Kenwood who changed our way of life by pioneering in 1949 the first blender which opened up a completely new era in food preparation. In a matter of seconds the blender brings to cooking a new and exciting range of tastes and flavours unequalled by any amount of chopping, whipping, mixing, beating, slicing.

The secret of getting the best out of your blender is never to put it away. The new Kenwood model is not only attractive in the kitchen but is ready for action twenty-four hours a day. It is about the most versatile kitchen aid that I have ever seen.

Early in my married life, as a time-pressed journalist, I learned to use my blender to the full. All I wanted then was a foolproof gadget that would fit into a galley-sized kitchen and work a miracle at the end of the day when my temper was frayed. The blender did it all. It makes delicious soup, fruit drinks, sauces, appetizers, relishes, salad dressings, puddings, soufflés, cocktails and even morning-after pick-me-ups.

It added a zest and glamour to quick inexpensive food and, for that matter, to my life! Because of its increased efficiency I find the new blender even more enjoyable to use. More important, it has become my husband's favourite kitchen toy.

Because of its low price, the blender is no longer

restricted to the well established household. Most families can afford one. And for the bride it must rate high up on her wedding list purely because of its usefulness.

The more you use the blender the more exciting your cooking becomes. For the best results, and to work to the timing given in this book for each recipe, you must gather round the blender all the ingredients before you begin so that once the machine is started you don't have to stop and wander off looking in cupboards. In this way, too, your cooking becomes more streamlined and professional. For instance, actual preparation time of soup is minimal. Cream of corn soup takes one minute, cream of watercress, which really does taste of watercress, takes thirty seconds and beetroot blender soup, served hot or cold, can be made in a wink. I doubt that a Russian could tell the difference between the blender's and the soup his mother made.

SOUPS

The blender opens up a whole new field in cold soups which add variety to the humblest summer meal and can be made and stored in the refrigerator for several days. Spanish gazpacho can be made in less than a minute. Cold jellied tomato soup or avocado soup are both appetizing as a first course for a special luncheon menu—and decorative. The blender also allows you to experiment with fruit soups which, served hot or cold, are favourites with children on the Continent and healthy for them during the winter months.

BABY FEEDING

The whole approach to feeding the baby has been re-thought since the blender took over in the kitchen. Even without a deep freeze it is possible to make and store baby food for several days at a fraction of the cost of the bought tins. In her first days home from hospital, tired and over-anxious, the mother can prepare her daily requirements and store them in sterilised bottles in the refrigerator. It saves time, separate calculations for each feed and washing up!

Once the vegetables have been cooked one only

has to add a little milk or bone stock and the blender does the rest in 20 to 30 seconds. Fruit provides the baby with the necessary vitamins and minerals for growth and development. Delicious 'afters' like banana, prune, apple or pear purée all take just half a minute to make in a busy morning.

PARTY SNACKS

With the invention of the blender we can be so much more original, and economical, in our approach to what the Americans call 'cocktail party dips' and sandwich spreads. They can be made in a matter of seconds, well ahead of the party, and again stored in the refrigerator until wanted. Home-made pâté from fresh chicken livers or liver sausage, rosy pink crab spread, frankfurter and sweet pickle or walnut and cheese spread will all become favourites with your guests.

Cake making becomes so much easier too with the help of your blender. This goes for real home-made ones as well as cake mixes. The chocolate angel pie or peppermint chiffon pie are imports from America that I am sure your family will enjoy.

HEALTH FOOD

With the health food craze well under way and more and more emphasis on slimming food and calorie-conscious diets, the blender is invaluable. Here you have a whole new range of flavours waiting to be tried . . . carrot blended with pineapple juice; watercress with lemon (a slimmer's special); fresh tomato with fresh mint. Served with crushed ice like a frappé, they take the boredom out of dieting. Runner bean salad, tomato aspic, pear and cottage cheese salad are all foods to tempt the slimmer and make their daily menu not only economical but interesting. In fact the blender can transform the whole salad world. In a matter of seconds you can make a creamy mayonnaise or piquant dressing. Cold ham mousse, chicken salad, rice bowl and cabbage salad and tuna mayonnaise ring are among the more unusual recipes you can try.

COCKTAIL DRINKS

For husbands, the range of drinks they can make is almost unlimited. Have the ingredients handy and with a few seconds in the kitchen while the guests are arriving the drinks are ready. Whisky Sour gets any party going while all the nostalgia of the nineteen-twenties comes flooding back if you serve such old favourites as Frozen Daiquiri or Tom Collins. Silver Fizz (based on gin) is one of the prettiest drinks that I have ever seen and Orange Blossom (gin, orange and white of egg) is delicious and decorative for a summer party.

These are just a few ideas selected from the following pages to illustrate how blender cooking brings a new philosophy to the kitchen, shattering old fashioned prejudices, presenting vast new possibilities.

This is what the blender cook book is about. It covers every aspect of cooking from soups to dessert and throws in lots of unexpected surprises like relishes and drinks. I promise that once you begin, you too will become a compulsive blender cook.

The Kenwood experimental kitchen in the company's modern factory at Havant near Portsmouth has tested every recipe so they really are foolproof and the most inexperienced of cooks can use them with confidence.

All the ingredients are available in normal well stocked grocery shops or supermarkets.

Have fun and happy blending.

Northleigh,   Gwen Robyns
Summer 1971

Basic Blender Hints

The following points will be invaluable when creating new recipes and when adapting well tried family favourites.

DRY INGREDIENTS
Bread and biscuit crumbs, chopped chocolate, nuts, fresh herbs, can all be prepared for use within a few seconds. Break the food into pieces small enough to pass through the hole in the lid. Switch on the blender and drop the food one piece at a time through the hole onto the revolving blades, keeping one hand over the opening. When the goblet is one-third full, empty and start again.

SOUPS
Use left-over foods. A variety of raw vegetables with stock and seasonings makes a good tasty soup. Blend everything together until the desired consistency is reached. The cooking time is so short that the maximum flavour and food value are retained.

PURÉES
Vegetables, soft raw fruits (tomatoes and strawberries) or cooked hard foods need no additional liquid. Half fill the goblet and switch on until a purée is reached. Cream soups, mousses and fruit fools are so simple when prepared this way.

DRINKS
The scope is unlimited. Simply place all ingredients, including ice, in the goblet and blend for a few seconds.

BABY FOODS
Add the cooked food to a little milk, butter or gravy and switch on. Stop during the process to scrape down from the sides.

With the use of the blender all kinds of delicious, tasty spreads can be made economically in a few seconds. Used in canapés or for sandwiches—open or closed—they make party food look colourful and festive. With the addition of a little liquid such as melted butter, various domestic sauces or mayonnaise left-overs can also be made into spreads for the family's supper or television snacks. Stored in the refrigerator they will keep for several days.

From the selection of thirty given here, Pâté Vite, Rich and Rosy Crab Spread and Sunshine Dip are especially suitable for cocktail parties.

Appetizers and Spreads

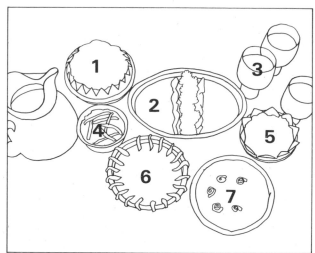

1   Apple Stuffed Edam
2   Pineapple Blue Cheese Dip
3   Red wine
4   Pronto Chicken Spread
5   Sunshine Dip
6   Shrimp Dip
7   Saucy Sardine Spread

Caviar Dip

A most elegant dip for special occasions. Celery hearts and radishes make interesting dippers

5 fluid ounce sour cream
3 tablespoons tomato purée
1 (2-ounce tin) caviar
1 teaspoon Worcestershire sauce
1 tablespoon lemon juice
Chopped parsley to garnish

Blend all ingredients for 10-15 seconds or until smooth. Serve with toast triangles.

Apple Stuffed Edam

For a party centre-piece, serve in a scooped-out Edam

½-pound Edam cheese (cubed)
1 medium apple (cored and cubed)
6 tablespoons cream
1 teaspoon lemon juice
Salt to taste

Blend all ingredients for 1 minute, stopping the motor to push the ingredients back onto blades when necessary. Place in dish and chill.

Tangy Cheese Spread

8-ounce cottage cheese
6 tablespoons single cream
1 teaspoon Worcestershire sauce
¼ clove garlic (peeled)
¼ teaspoon basil
Dash Tabasco sauce

Blend all ingredients for 30-35 seconds, stopping motor to push ingredients back onto blades when necessary.
Serve as an appetizer spread for sandwiches, or chill and form into a ball.

Saucy Sardine Spread

Use fresh vegetables—celery, radishes, carrots—for dippers

8-ounce cottage cheese
8-ounce tinned sardines (drained)
1 tablespoon prepared horseradish
½ clove garlic
½ teaspoon Worcestershire sauce
4 tablespoons mayonnaise (*see* page 107)
2 sticks celery

Blend all ingredients for 30 seconds or until smooth, stopping motor to push ingredients back onto blades when necessary.

Shrimp Dip

1 (4½-5 ounce) tin shrimps (drained)
6 tablespoons mayonnaise
1½-ounce Cheddar cheese (cubed)
3 tablespoons milk
1 small onion (sliced)
1 teaspoon Worcestershire sauce

Reserve a few shrimps for garnish. Blend all ingredients for 1 minute, stopping motor to push ingredients back onto blades when necessary. Chill. Garnish with reserved shrimps.

Sunshine Dip

Try this dip on tomato slices or over hot cooked vegetables

3 hard boiled eggs (peeled and diced)
1 (3-ounce) packet cream cheese (cubed)
2 tablespoons single cream
2 tablespoons mayonnaise
1 teaspoon prepared mustard
1 tablespoon coarsely chopped green pepper
1 teaspoon vinegar

Blend all ingredients for 30 seconds or until smooth.

Pronto Chicken Spread

For sandwiches or canapés

4-ounce cooked chicken (cubed)
3 tablespoons mayonnaise
1-ounce coarsely chopped green pepper
1 tomato
1 stick celery (sliced)
Salt to taste

Blend all ingredients for 45 seconds, stopping motor to push ingredients back onto blades when necessary.

Pineapple Blue Cheese Dip

Also good as a salad dressing, especially for fruits

8-ounce cream cheese (cubed)
1 (8-ounce) tin crushed pineapple (drained)
5-ounce blue cheese (cubed)
1 tablespoon chopped chives

Blend all ingredients for 60 seconds or until smooth, stopping motor to push ingredients back onto blades when necessary. Chill.

Bacon Dip

Try this also as a sauce for cooked vegetables or baked potatoes

6 slices of bacon (cooked and diced—
   approx. 6-ounce)
5 fluid ounce sour cream
3 tablespoons mayonnaise
1 slice onion
$\frac{1}{4}$ lemon (peeled)
1 tablespoon parsley sprigs

Blend all ingredients for about 30 seconds or until smooth.

Pâté Vite

$1\frac{1}{2}$-ounce walnuts
5 tablespoons mayonnaise
1 tablespoon sherry
$\frac{1}{2}$ teaspoon nutmeg
$\frac{1}{2}$-pound liver sausage (cubed)
1 hard boiled egg (peeled)
Salt to taste

Chop the nuts in the blender. Add mayonnaise, sherry and seasoning. Blend for a further 10 seconds.

With motor running, add the liver sausage a cube at a time. Continue blending till smooth, stopping motor to push ingredients back onto blades when necessary.

Pack into a $\frac{1}{2}$ pint mould and chill. Unmould onto serving plate. Separate egg and chop the white and yolk separately, about 3-5 seconds each.

Garnish top of pâté with ring of chopped yolk and white.

Walnutty Cheese Spread,
Bacon Dip and
Shrimp Ball

14

Blended Avocado Dip

3 medium sized avocados (peeled and
  cubed)
1 medium tomato (blanched and cubed)
1 small onion (sliced)
2 tablespoons lemon or lime juice
Salt to taste
Dash of hot pepper sauce
2 tablespoons mayonnaise

Blend all ingredients for 30 seconds or until
smooth, stopping motor to push ingredients back
onto blades when necessary.

Chutney Cheese Spread

1 (4-ounce) packet of cream cheese
  (cubed)
2-ounce chutney
1 tablespoon lemon juice
½ teaspoon curry powder
⅛ teaspoon dry mustard
Salt to taste
Dessicated coconut

Blend first 6 ingredients for 45 seconds, stopping
motor to push ingredients back onto blades when
necessary.
Chill. Garnish with dessicated coconut.

Blended Avocado Dip,
Rich and Rosy Crab Spread,
Frankfurter Spread,
Savoury Salmon Spread
and Egg Salad Spread

15

Egg Salad Spread

5 tablespoons mayonnaise
1 tablespoon chili sauce
Salt to taste
8 hard boiled eggs
Sliced pimento (fresh)
Stuffed olives

Blend mayonnaise, chilli sauce and salt for 5 seconds. Add eggs, pimento and olives and blend for a further 30 seconds, stopping motor to push the ingredients back onto blades when necessary.

Savoury Salmon Spread

8-ounce cottage cheese
1 (7¾-ounce) tin salmon (drained)
3 tablespoons single cream
1 slice onion
1 teaspoon chopped chives
½ teaspoon paprika
Salt and pepper to taste
Dash hot pepper sauce (e.g. Tabasco)

Blend all ingredients for 30 seconds or until smooth. Chill.

Rich and Rosy Crab Spread

1 (7½-ounce) tin of crab meat
2 fluid ounce single cream
1 tablespoon prepared horseradish

Blend all ingredients for 30 seconds or until smooth, stopping motor to push ingredients back onto blades when necessary.
This can be heated with cheese for an extra rich spread.

Frankfurter Spread

5 Frankfurters (sliced)
4 tablespoons mayonnaise
16 stuffed olives (sliced)
5 tablespoons pickle
1 teaspoon prepared mustard

Blend all ingredients for 45 seconds, stopping motor to push ingredients back onto blades when necessary.

Walnutty Cheese Spread

1 (8-ounce) packet cream cheese
1½-ounce walnuts
2-ounce chopped green pepper
4 tablespoons double cream
Salt to taste

Blend all ingredients for 30 seconds, stopping motor to push ingredients back onto blades when necessary.

Ham and Mushroom Dunk

3-ounce cooked ham (cubed)
1 (4-ounce) tin of mushrooms (drained)
3 tablespoons chutney
3 tablespoons mayonnaise
¼ teaspoon paprika

Blend all ingredients for 45 seconds or until smooth, stopping motor to push ingredients back onto blades when necessary.

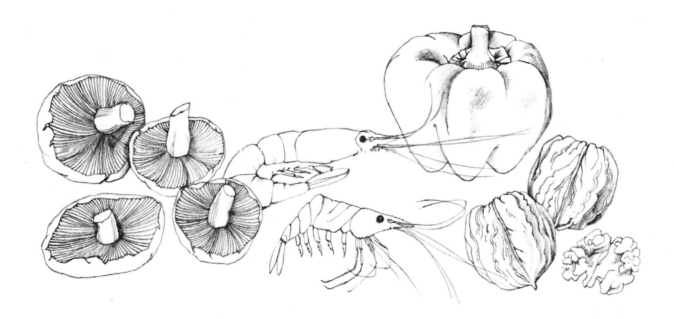

Shrimp Sandwich Spread

1 (4½-ounce) tin shrimps (drained)
2 tablespoons mayonnaise
2-ounce sliced celery
1-ounce coarsely chopped green pepper
1 tablespoon lemon juice
1 teaspoon prepared horseradish
Salt to taste

Chop all ingredients for 45 seconds, stopping motor to push ingredients back onto blades when necessary.
Spread on bread slices or toast rounds.

Shrimp Ball

1 (4½-5-ounce) tin shrimps (drained)
½ small onion (sliced)
1½-ounce margarine or butter (softened)
3 tablespoons mayonnaise
1 tablespoon lemon juice
Salt to taste
4 tablespoons chopped parsley

Blend shrimps first until finely chopped in the blender. Add all remaining ingredients except parsley and blend for 30 seconds or until smooth, stopping motor to push ingredients back onto blades when necessary.
Chill thoroughly, then shape into a ball. Roll shrimp ball in parsley to coat thoroughly, then chill again.

Cheese Duo Dip

Top a fresh fruit salad with a spoonful of this dip

8-ounce cream cheese (cubed)
8-ounce blue cheese (cubed)
6 tablespoons evaporated milk
$\frac{1}{4}$ clove garlic

Blend all ingredients for 45 seconds, stopping motor to push ingredients back onto blades when necessary.

Garlic Dip

Top a steak or baked potato with a big spoonful of this delicious dip

3 fluid ounce milk
2 teaspoons Worcestershire sauce
1 teaspoon paprika
$\frac{1}{2}$ clove garlic
1 teaspoon vinegar
8-ounce cream cheese (cubed)

Blend milk, Worcestershire sauce, paprika, garlic and vinegar for 10 seconds. With the motor running add the cheese a cube at a time through the opening in the lid. Continue blending until smooth.

Ham Dunk

4-ounce ham (cubed)
3-ounce cream cheese (cubed)
1 slice onion
1 tablespoon parsley sprigs
1$\frac{1}{2}$ teaspoons Worcestershire sauce

Blend all ingredients for 30 seconds or until smooth, stopping motor to push ingredients back onto blades when necessary.

Cream Anchovy Dip

Remember this recipe for a great Beef Fondue sauce

3 tablespoons mayonnaise
3 tablespoons double cream
1 slice onion
1 tablespoon parsley sprigs
1 tablespoon anchovy paste
6-ounce cream cheese (cubed)

Blend mayonnaise, cream, onion, parsley and anchovy paste for 15 seconds. With motor running add cheese a cube at a time through opening in the middle of the lid. Continue mixing until smooth.

Tasty Tuna Dip

1 (7-ounce) tin Tuna (drained)
6 tablespoons mayonnaise
1-ounce chopped onion
1-ounce coarsely chopped green pepper
1 stalk celery (sliced)
1 small carrot
1 teaspoon Worcestershire sauce
Salt to taste

Blend all ingredients for 45 seconds or until smooth, stopping motor to push ingredients back onto blades when necessary.

Ribbon Sandwich Loaves

*A great centre-piece and main dish
for a lunch—making 2 loaves*

1 unsliced white sandwich loaf
3-4-ounce butter or margarine (softened)
Curried Egg filling (*see* following recipe)
Avocado filling (*see* p. 20)
Ham filling (*see* p. 20)
2 (8-ounce) packets cream cheese (cubed)
¼ pint sour cream
2 tablespoons lemon juice
parsley sprigs and radish flowers or
  stuffed olives for garnish

Trim crusts from bread. Cut the loaf into 8 slices
lengthwise and arrange 2 slices on a chopping
board side by side to form the bottom tiers of the
2 'loaves'.

Spread with some of the softened butter and then
with the Curried Egg filling. Top each loaf with
another long slice of bread; spread with butter
and then with a layer of Avocado filling. Top each
loaf with another slice of bread; spread with
butter and then with a layer of Ham filling. Top
each loaf with the top layer of bread.

Blend the cream cheese, sour cream and lemon
juice, stopping motor to push ingredients back
onto blades when necessary.

Frost finish the loaves with cream cheese frosting,
reserving some of the frosting to pipe borders
with piping tube if desired. Garnish with parsley
sprigs, radish flowers or stuffed olives.

Curried Egg Filling

4 hard-boiled eggs
3 tablespoons mayonnaise
½ teaspoon curry powder

Blend all ingredients for 45 seconds, stopping motor to push ingredients back onto blades when necessary.

Avocado Filling

2 avocados (peeled and sliced)
1 tablespoon French dressing or
    mayonnaise
1 tablespoon lemon juice

Blend all ingredients for 30 seconds, stopping motor to push ingredients back onto blades when necessary.

Ham Filling

4-ounce diced ham
2 sticks celery
3 tablespoons mayonnaise

Blend all ingredients for 60 seconds, stopping motor to push ingredients back onto blades when necessary.

Mixed Cheese Dip

Slice apples and pears to use as dippers here

8-ounce cottage cheese
4-ounce Cheddar cheese (cubed)
3-ounce cream cheese (cubed)
8 tablespoons double cream
Salt to taste
⅛ teaspoon paprika

Blend all ingredients for 60 seconds, stopping motor to push ingredients back onto blades when necessary.

Ham and Cheese Bites

Tasty for appetizers or with a salad

2 dozen small baked biscuits
4-ounce ham
2-ounce Cheddar cheese (cubed)
1 egg
1 slice onion coarsely chopped
3 tablespoons mayonnaise

Blend all ingredients, except biscuits, for 45 seconds or until smooth, stopping motor to push ingredients back onto blades when necessary. Spread a little filling on a biscuit and put another on top. Place on a baking sheet and cook at 400° F/Reg 6 for 5 minutes until hot.

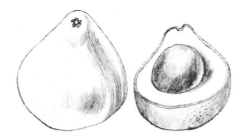

With your blender a whole new experience in drink-mixing awaits you. Cocktails are especially good when mixed in the blender as it gives an even blending and crushes the ice into fragments. For smooth, ice cold drinks strain immediately into glasses that have been chilled. For special effect dip the rims of the glasses in coloured sugar before putting them in the refrigerator.

Few husbands can resist the temptation of trying out not only the well known and trusted cocktails but inventing their own. Silver Fizz is one of the prettiest drinks for a summer party, while Brandy Egg Nog is guaranteed to get any winter party swinging.

For slimmers and non-alcohol drinkers we have included thirteen really delicious fruity drinks. The Gelatine Pick-Me-Up really does work if you are feeling below par. Doctors recommend this one especially if your finger nails need strengthening.

Drinks

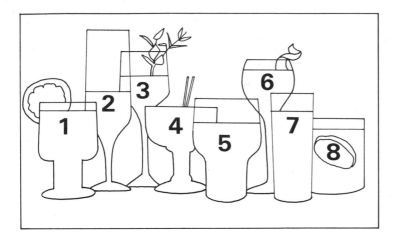

1 Orange Blossom
2 Sherry Flip
3 Emerald Fizz
4 Frozen Daiquiri
5 Brandy Egg Nog
6 Silver Fizz
7 Tom Collins
8 Whisky Sour

Orange Blossom

6 fluid ounce gin
4 fluid ounce orange juice
1 tablespoon lemon juice
1 level tablespoon sugar
2 ice cubes

Blend all ingredients for 15 seconds. Strain if desired.

Frozen Daiquiri

8 fluid ounce rum
2 fluid ounce concentrated lime juice
10 ice cubes (practice will tell you the
    amount to use)

Place all ingredients in the goblet and blend for 30 seconds or until slushy. Serve at once.

Sherry Flip

A lightning pick-me-up

2 egg yolks
3 fluid ounce sherry (use brandy if pre-
    ferred)
2 teaspoon sugar

Blend all ingredients for 10 seconds. Serve in a wine glass. Sprinkle with nutmeg.

Whisky Sour

Frosty, cold and frothy from the blender

8 fluid ounce whisky
3 fluid ounce lemon juice
2 level tablespoons sugar
2 ice cubes

Blend all ingredients for 20 seconds. Strain into glasses. Garnish with a lemon slice and maraschino cherry.

Tom or Rum Collins

1½ fluid ounce gin or rum
1½ fluid ounce lime or lemon juice
1 tablespoon powdered sugar
2 ice cubes
Soda water (chilled)

Blend gin or rum, lime or lemon juice, sugar and ice for 15 seconds. Strain into a tall chilled glass and top with soda water. Decorate with a lime or lemon slice and a maraschino cherry if desired.

Brandy Egg Nog

Rich and creamy. A necessity for a winter get-together

2 eggs (separated)
¼ pint brandy or whisky
1 fluid ounce dark rum (optional)
4 fluid ounce cold milk
½-ounce sugar
4 fluid ounce double cream

Blend egg yolks for 5 seconds. Add brandy, rum, milk and blend for a further 15 seconds. Pour into a chilled bowl. Whisk egg whites until foamy. Gradually add sugar and beat to stiff peaks. Whisk cream until it reaches 'piping' consistency. Fold egg whites and cream into brandy mixture. Sprinkle with nutmeg if desired.

Stinger

7½ fluid ounce brandy
3 fluid ounce crème de menthe
1½ fluid ounce lime juice
4 ice cubes

Blend all ingredients for 15 seconds and strain if desired.

Silver Fizz

1½ fluid ounce gin
1½ fluid ounce lemon juice
1 egg white
1 teaspoon sugar
1-2 ice cubes
Soda water (chilled)

Blend the first 5 ingredients for 15 seconds. Strain if desired into a glass and top up with soda water.

Emerald Fizz

1½ fluid ounce gin
1½ fluid ounce lemon juice
1 egg white
1 teaspoon crème de menthe
1 teaspoon sugar
2 ice cubes

Blend all ingredients for 30 seconds and strain if desired.

Orange Frappé

1 (6-ounce) tin frozen orange juice concentrate
2 trays ice cubes
3 fluid ounce bourbon, gin or vodka

Blend all ingredients for about 1 minute or until
slushy. Mound in glasses and serve at once.

Cherry Whiz

¾ pint unsweetened pineapple juice
   (chilled)
6 ounce stoned red tart cherries, fresh or
   canned
1 slice lemon

Blend all ingredients for 1 minute. Pour contents
of blender through sieve if desired.
Pour over cracked ice or add 3 ice cubes and blend
a few seconds longer.

Pineapple Mint Whip

¾ pint cold milk
12-ounce drained pineapple chunks
   (chilled)
1 sprig fresh mint

Blend all ingredients for 1-1½ minutes. Serve
immediately.

Choco Mint Float

4-8 drops peppermint according to taste
1 pint milk
1 family block of vanilla or chocolate ice-
   cream (cut into cubes)
Green food colouring
(red colouring looks more attractive with
   chocolate ice-cream)
2-ounce chocolate (grated)

Blend peppermint essence and milk for 10 seconds.
Add ice-cream and colouring and blend for a
further 30-40 seconds, until smooth.
Sprinkle with grated chocolate before serving.

Kenwood Lemonade

*One lemon makes a whole jugful
of lemonade*

1 lemon
2 tablespoons sugar
6 ice cubes
1¼ pints cold water

Thin-skinned lemons are best for this purpose.
Place lemon, sugar and ice in the goblet, top up to
the 1½ pint level with cold water, and turn on for
10 seconds. Strain into a jug.
To serve, add one or two more ice cubes and float
thin slices of lemon in the drink.

Kenwood Lemonade,
Orange Frappé,
Choco Mint Float,
Cherry Whiz and
Pineapple Mint Whip

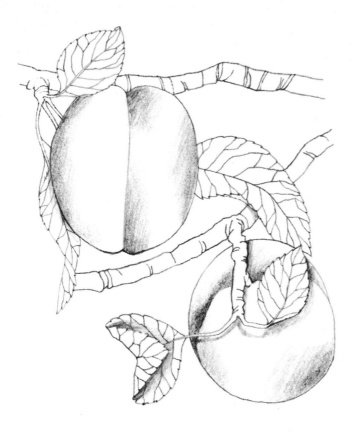

Moscow Chocolate

½ pint hot water
1-ounce chocolate (plain)
2 tablespoons sugar
¾ pint hot coffee (black)
8 fluid ounce milk
¼ teaspoon vanilla essence

Blend hot water, chocolate and sugar for 30 seconds. Pour into a saucepan along with the remaining ingredients and heat until piping hot (do not boil). Stir before serving.

Apricot Shake

A golden creamy drink popular with all ages

¾ pint cold milk   Soak apricots in
3-ounce dried apricots   milk overnight
1 tablespoon sugar
¼ teaspoon vanilla essence

Blend all ingredients for 1-1½ minutes. Pour into chilled glasses. Decorate with dried or tinned apricots if desired.

Fresh Rhubarb Cocktail

12 fluid ounce unsweetened pineapple
    juice (chilled)
4-ounce raw rhubarb (diced)
1 tablespoon honey
9 ice cubes

Blend all ingredients for 1 minute. Strain through a sieve and serve immediately.

Orange Glow

½ pint cold milk
3 fluid ounce orange juice (fresh)
1 orange (peeled and quartered)
1 lemon (peeled and quartered)
1 tablespoon sugar
4 ice cubes

Blend all ingredients for 60 seconds or until smooth. Sieve if desired.

Raspberry Fizz

4-ounce fresh or frozen raspberries
2 fluid ounce fresh orange juice
2 teaspoons lemon juice
1 level tablespoon sugar
½ tray ice cubes
1 pint soda water (chilled)

Blend raspberries, orange and lemon juice and sugar for 10 seconds. Add ice and blend for a further 15 seconds. Pour into 4 chilled glasses and fill with soda water. Garnish with sprigs of fresh mint.

Fresh Vegetable Cocktail

You can call this a 'Zombie' to give to your teenagers. They'll never guess it's good for them

¾ pint unsweetened pineapple juice (chilled)
1 small carrot (sliced)
1 stalk celery (sliced)
¼ cucumber (peeled and sliced)
1 slice lemon

Blend all ingredients for 1 minute. Add 3 ice cubes and blend for a few seconds longer.
This cocktail may be sieved if desired.

Gelatine Pick-Me-Up

Helps in dieting and strengthening finger nails

1 envelope unflavoured gelatine
6 fluid ounce cold or hot liquid (orange, tomato or other juices, milk, water, broth or bouillon)

Blend gelatine and liquid for 10 seconds if liquid is cold, and 40 seconds if liquid is hot. Drink at once.

Four Fruit Whiz

Change or add fresh, tinned or frozen fruits of your choosing and create your own flavour blends

¾ pint unsweetened pineapple juice (chilled)
1 orange (peeled and quartered)
½ apple (cored and sliced)
½ pear (cored and sliced)

Blend all ingredients for 45 seconds. Pour over ice cubes to serve.

Multi-Mix Drink

Here's a health drink which is delightfully refreshing

½ pint apple juice
9 ice cubes
3 fluid ounce fresh orange juice
3-ounce fresh/canned fruit of your choice
½ carrot sliced
1 egg
1 celery stalk (sliced)
¼ banana (peeled)
2 leaves of spinach
12 almonds
1 teaspoon raisins
2 parsley sprigs

Blend all ingredients for 1-1½ minutes. Serve immediately.

Sunny Slipper

¾ pint unsweetened pineapple juice (chilled)
1 medium carrot
1 orange (peeled and quartered)
1 tablespoon seedless raisins

Blend all ingredients for 1 minute. Add 3 ice cubes and blend for a few seconds longer.

Mint Punch

6 sprigs of fresh mint
6-ounce sugar
¾ pint water
¾ pint lemon juice
1-2 drops green food colouring
1 quart ginger ale (chilled)

Blend mint, sugar and water for 15 seconds. Simmer for 5 minutes. Strain then add lemon juice and colouring. Chill thoroughly. Gently mix with ginger ale to serve. Decorate with additional mint sprigs.

Mocha Delight

1 pint cold milk
1 tablespoon sugar
1½ level tablespoons instant coffee
½ family block chocolate ice-cream (cut into cubes)

Blend all ingredients together for 15-20 seconds. Serve immediately in chilled glasses.

Strawberry Frost

6-ounce fresh or frozen strawberries
8 fluid ounce fresh orange juice
1-2 tablespoons sugar
9 ice cubes

Blend all ingredients for 1 minute or until smooth.

Left, Mint Punch

Opposite, Watercress Whiz,
Souper Nog and
Minted Ice Tea

Watercress Whiz

A quick nutritious cool drink for summer

½ pint unsweetened pineapple juice
  (chilled)
1 bunch watercress (washed)

Blend all ingredients for 1 minute. Add 3 ice cubes and blend for a few seconds longer.
Decorate with additional watercress sprigs if desired.

Souper Nog

1 (10½-ounce) tin tomato soup
½ pint milk
1 egg
½ teaspoon nutmeg

Blend all ingredients for 15 seconds. Chill or add 2 ice cubes and blend for a further few seconds.

Minted Ice Tea

Fresh and true flavours. You'll make this all summer long

4 sprigs of mint
1 lemon (peeled and quartered)
1 (1 in.) strip lemon peel
2 tablespoons sugar
3 pints hot tea

Blend mint, lemon peel, sugar and ¼ pint of the hot tea for 15 seconds. Pour into a jug or container and pour the hot tea over, allowing for this to stand for 20 minutes. Strain into a jug and chill thoroughly.

Cherry Vanilla Float

1 (4-ounce) jar maraschino cherries
1 pint cold milk
1 block vanilla ice-cream

Reserve 4 cherries to decorate. Blend remaining cherries, syrup and milk for 25-30 seconds together with the ice-cream. Sieve if desired and serve.

Strawberry-Banana Milk Shake

$\frac{3}{4}$ pint milk
3-ounce vanilla ice-cream (cubed)
1 banana (peeled and sliced)
4-ounce strawberries (hulled)

Blend all ingredients for 45 seconds. Sieve or leave, according to taste.

Double Raspberry Soda

A perfect Bridge party refresher

6-ounce frozen raspberries (partially
   thawed)
6 fluid ounce milk
Small block of Raspberry Ripple (cubed)
8 fluid ounce soda water

Blend raspberries and milk for 15 seconds. Strain if desired. Add ice-cream and blend for further 30 seconds. Pour into glasses and top up with soda water.

Pineapple-Orange Frost

1 pint cold milk
Family block pineapple ice-cream (cubed)
1 orange (peeled and quartered)

A vanilla block can be used but in this case use 3 oranges rather than 1.
Blend all ingredients for 30 seconds or until smooth. Strain if desired. Decorate with a slice of orange and fresh or canned pineapple chunks.

Best Banana Milk Shake

8 fluid ounce cold milk
1 banana (peeled and sliced)
4 ice cubes
1 tablespoon honey

Blend all ingredients for 1 minute. Sprinkle with nutmeg if desired.

Fruit Nut Milk Shake

$\frac{3}{4}$-pint cold milk
8-10 canned peach slices or 2 fresh peach
   halves
1 banana (peeled and sliced)
2 stoned dates
2 tablespoons almonds

Blend all ingredients for 1 minute. Sieve or leave according to taste. Pour into chilled glasses.

Soup is perhaps the most satisfying thing to make in the blender. In a matter of seconds you can produce delicious soups with exciting flavours that would take hours to make any other way.

Try the celery soup which is equally delicious cold or hot. Including cooking time, it can be made in three minutes. Onion soup, a stand-by of the French kitchen, can be made with your blender in just over five minutes.

Cold soups, which are becoming much more popular, add a touch of sophistication to any dinner party. Frosty Crab soup, which takes only 15 seconds to make, is a marvellous way to begin a dinner party.

Soups

1 Beetroot Blend Soup
2 Swedish Cherry Soup
3 Avocado Soup
4 Curry Cream Soup
5 Cream of Mushroom Soup

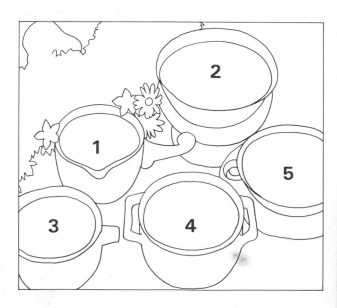

Swedish Cherry Soup

*A flavour surprise for first course
or dessert*

1 (1-pound) tin Morello cherries
3-ounce sugar
$\frac{1}{8}$ orange (thin orange portion of peel and
   fruit)
2 teaspoons cornflour
$\frac{1}{4}$ teaspoon cinnamon
Salt to taste

Blend all ingredients for 15 seconds or until
smooth. Pour into saucepan and cook, stirring
over a medium heat until the mixture begins to
boil.
Simmer gently for 2 minutes stirring all the time.
Serve hot or chill thoroughly and serve cold. Top
with a tablespoonful of soured cream if desired.

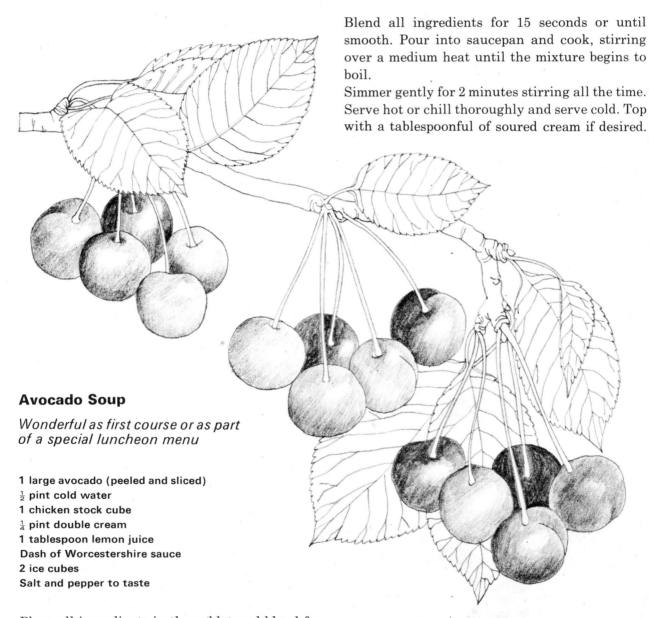

Avocado Soup

*Wonderful as first course or as part
of a special luncheon menu*

1 large avocado (peeled and sliced)
$\frac{1}{2}$ pint cold water
1 chicken stock cube
$\frac{1}{4}$ pint double cream
1 tablespoon lemon juice
Dash of Worcestershire sauce
2 ice cubes
Salt and pepper to taste

Place all ingredients in the goblet and blend for
30 seconds. Chill thoroughly before serving.

Cream of Mushroom Soup

Garnish with a spoonful of lightly salted whipped cream and a piece of pimento, or with thin, sauté mushroom slices

¼ lb. fresh mushrooms (sliced)
1 ounce butter or margarine
¾ pint milk
1 slice onion
2 level tablespoons plain flour
1 ounce butter or margarine
Salt to taste
⅛ teaspoon pepper

Sauté mushrooms in 1 ounce butter until tender. Blend milk, onion, flour, butter, salt and pepper for 5 seconds. Turn into saucepan, add mushrooms and heat, stirring until the soup boils. Simmer for 2-3 minutes. Serve piping hot.
You may substitute 1 (4 ounce) tin mushrooms and liquid for fresh mushrooms and 1 ounce butter.

Curry Cream Soup

Delicate flavours, deliciously blended

1 (10½-ounce) tin consommé
½ pint water
1 medium onion (quartered)
1 medium apple (peeled, cored and quartered)
½ teaspoon curry powder
¼ teaspoon paprika
¼ pint double cream
Apple slices for garnish

Blend all ingredients, except the cream, for 30 seconds. Add cream and blend for a further 5 seconds. Pour into saucepan and heat until piping hot.

Garnish with croûtons or apple slices which have been brushed with lemon juice to prevent them from 'browning'.

Beetroot Blend Soup

Serve hot or cold

1 (1-pound) tin beetroots (undrained)
¾ pint milk
1 stick celery (sliced)
1 slice onion
Salt to taste

Blend all ingredients for 45 seconds. Chill thoroughly or pour into saucepan and heat until piping hot.
Garnish with sour cream and chives.

Celery Soup

Refreshing cold and delicious hot

¾ pint milk
4 sticks celery (sliced)
1 slice onion
1 level tablespoon plain flour
6 peppercorns
salt to taste

Blend all ingredients for 1 minute. Pour into a saucepan and cook, stirring allow it to simmer for 2 minutes. Serve hot or chilled.

New Old Fashioned Soup

So fresh the vegetables are still crisp

2 (10½-ounce) tins consommé
1 (8-ounce) tin tomato soup
½ pint water
3-ounce potato (diced and peeled)
1-ounce carrot (sliced)
1 stalk celery
2 slices onion
½-ounce diced green pepper
Salt to taste
½ teaspoon basil

Blend all ingredients except soups for 10 seconds. Turn into saucepan with soup and bring to the boil. Lower heat and simmer for 5 minutes.

Cold Cucumber Soup

1 pint cold milk
1 medium cucumber (peeled and
    roughly chopped)
4 large sprigs of parsley
1 level teaspoon salt
Dash of pepper

Place all ingredients in the goblet and blend for
30-45 seconds. Chill thoroughly. Stir before
serving.
Garnish with thin slices of cucumber.

Cream of Corn Soup

Garden fresh flavour in seconds

¾ pint milk
1 (1-pound) tin whole kernel corn
    (undrained)
Salt to taste
Dash Tabasco sauce

Blend all ingredients for 1 minute. Turn into
saucepan and heat until piping hot.

Ten Second French Onion Soup

1¼ pint hot water (or stock)
3 beef stock cubes
3 medium onions (quartered)
½-ounce butter

Blend all ingredients for 10 seconds. Turn into a
saucepan, bring to the boil and then simmer for
5 minutes.
To serve French style top each serving of soup
with a slice of toasted French bread, sprinkled
generously with grated cheese.

Iowa Corn Chowder

$\frac{3}{4}$ pint milk
1 (1-pound) tin whole kernel corn
   (undrained)
1 medium potato (cooked and cubed)
4 slices bacon (cooked and crisp)
2 slices onion
Salt to taste
6 peppercorns
Dash hot pepper sauce

Blend all ingredients for 1 minute. Turn into saucepan and heat until piping hot.

Chicken Vegetable Soup

$1\frac{1}{4}$ pint water
2 chicken stock cubes
3-4-ounce cooked chicken (cubed)
$1\frac{1}{2}$-ounce carrot (sliced)
1-2 sticks celery (sliced)
1 slice onion
Salt to taste
$\frac{1}{8}$ teaspoon pepper

Blend all ingredients for 10 seconds. Pour into saucepan and heat until piping hot.

Cream of Watercress Soup

$\frac{3}{4}$ pint cold water
1 chicken stock cube
$\frac{1}{4}$ pint double cream
1 bunch watercress (washed)
1 rounded tablespoon plain flour

Place all ingredients in the goblet and blend for 30 seconds. Turn the soup into a saucepan and heat, stirring occasionally until it boils. Allow the soup to boil for 2 minutes and then serve piping hot.

Celery and Corn Cream Soup

1 (1-pound) tin whole kernel corn (drained)
$\frac{1}{2}$ pint milk
4 sticks celery (sliced)
1 teaspoon salt
8 peppercorns

Blend all ingredients for 1 minute. Pour into saucepan and heat until piping hot.

Jellied Mushroom Soup

2 (10$\frac{1}{2}$-ounce) tins consommé
$\frac{1}{2}$-pound mushrooms (coarsely chopped)
4 fluid ounce water
1 packet gelatin
1 (2 in.) piece lemon peel
$\frac{1}{4}$ lemon (peeled)
2 fluid ounce white wine
Salt and pepper to taste
1 carton plain yogurt
Chopped chives for garnish

Simmer consommé and mushrooms for 20 minutes. Blend together water, gelatin, lemon peel and lemon for 20 seconds. Add consommé, mushrooms, wine, salt and pepper to taste, and blend for a further 10 seconds.
Chill until served. Garnish with yogurt and chopped chives.

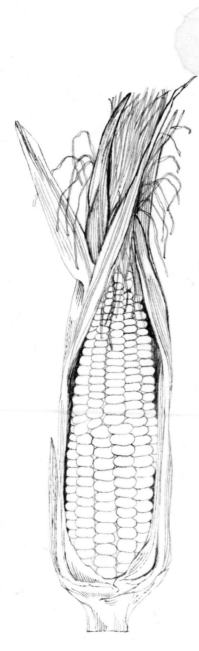

Surprise Soup

1 (10-ounce) packet frozen spinach
¾ pint milk
1 large cooked potato (diced)
1 slice onion
2 teaspoons Worcestershire sauce
½ level teaspoon salt
Good pinch nutmeg
½ clove garlic

Cook the spinach in a small amount of boiling salt water for 5 minutes. Drain the spinach and place in the goblet with the rest of the ingredients. Blend for 30 seconds. Return to saucepan and heat until piping hot. A little sherry can be stirred in before serving if desired.
Garnish with chopped parsley.

Gazpacho

Spain's famous soup salad

4 tomatoes (skinned and quartered)
¼ green pepper (seeded and cubed)
½ cucumber (peeled and sliced)
½ onion (sliced)
2 stalks celery (sliced)
3 parsley sprigs
⅓ clove garlic (peeled)
¼ pint cold water
1 tablespoon tarragon vinegar
2 tablespoons olive or salad oil
Salt to taste
½ teaspoon Worcestershire sauce
¾ teaspoon pepper

Blend all ingredients for 15 seconds. Chill thoroughly before serving.

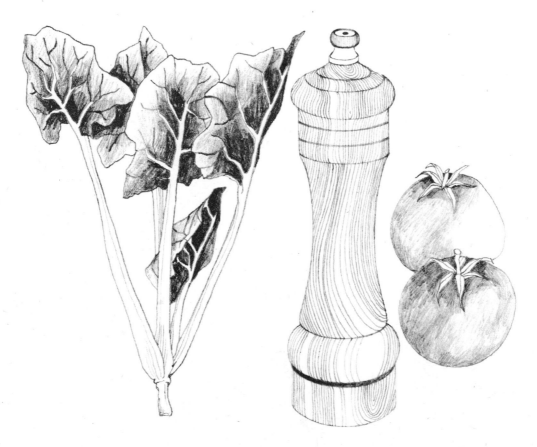

Gazpacho

Oyster Stew

¾ pint milk
1½-ounce plain flour
1-ounce butter
2 teaspoons Worcestershire sauce
½ level teaspoon salt
1 (8-ounce) tin oysters (undrained)

Blend milk, flour, butter, Worcestershire sauce and salt for 30 seconds. Turn into a saucepan and bring to the boil, stirring occasionally. Allow to boil for 2-3 minutes. Stir in oysters and liquid and serve piping hot.

Montreal Cheese Soup

¾ pint milk
1 chicken stock cube
½ pint water
4 ounce Cheddar cheese (cubed)
1-ounce carrots (sliced)
1 stick celery (sliced)
1 slice onion
2 level tablespoons plain flour
Salt to taste
6 peppercorns
¼ teaspoon nutmeg

Blend all ingredients for 30 seconds. Pour into saucepan and heat until boiling. Simmer for 2 minutes stirring all the time. Serve piping hot.

Frosty Crab Soup

1¼ pint milk
1 (5-ounce) tin crab
1 small cucumber (peeled and sliced)
½ bunch watercress
1 teaspoon sugar
1 teaspoon prepared mustard
Salt to taste

Blend all ingredients for 15 seconds. Chill thoroughly. Garnish with chopped chives.

Choice Cream Soup

½ pint milk
4 ounce of any of the following: sliced raw or cooked carrots, cooked broccoli, cooked asparagus, cooked cauliflower, cooked green beans, cooked mixed vegetables, cooked corn
½ pint water
3 level tablespoons plain flour
1½-ounce butter or margarine
1 chicken stock cube
Salt to taste
1 teaspoon Worcestershire sauce

Blend all ingredients for 30-45 seconds. Turn into saucepan and bring to the boil. Simmer for 2 minutes stirring all the time. Serve piping hot.

These recipes are fun to make and many of them can be prepared in the morning for cooking or heating up when the family comes home in the evening.

With chicken one of the cheapest meats in the shops there are several recipes here that will not spoil even if the family is late. Country Chicken with its sauce of Tomatoes, Green pepper and onion, flavoured with that fragrant Italian herb oregano, or sweet basil, is easy to make.

If you like unusual flavours try the Java Pork Kabobs. These can be prepared before the guests come and grilled for 15 minutes during the first course. Indian Lamb Skewers, laced with canned apricot halves, is an exotic dish but if you prefer your lamb simpler try the Marinated Leg of Lamb—a classical French recipe.

Lunch and Supper Dishes

Lamb Kebabs

Baked Ham

Baked Ham

Weigh the joint and calculate the time required for cooking, allowing 15 minutes to the pound plus 15 minutes for a joint greater than 12 pounds, and 20 minutes per pound plus 20 minutes for a joint smaller than 12 pounds.

Soak the joint overnight in cold water. Rinse it, put it into a saucepan with enough water to completely cover the joint. Add a Bouquet Garni. Bring the joint slowly to the boil and simmer for half the time required. Remove the ham from the liquid and dry it before covering it with tin foil. Place it in a roasting tin and cook at 325° F/Reg 3 for the remaining time, less 20 minutes. Take the ham from the oven, remove the tin foil and skin, and score the fat in diamonds. Insert whole cloves and glaze with Orange Sauce, or Cherry Sauce (*see* this page). Put back in the oven and cook for remaining 20 minutes to brown.

Sour Cream Sauce

$\frac{1}{4}$ pint water
3 tablespoons plain flour
$\frac{1}{4}$ teaspoon marjoram
$\frac{1}{4}$ teaspoon dill seed
$\frac{1}{4}$ pint sour cream

Blend water, flour and marjoram for 10 seconds. Cook and stir over a medium heat until thick. Add dill seed and sour cream. Heat, stirring gently but do not boil. If serving with a meat dish the blend of flour, water and marjoram could be placed with the meat drippings and cooked with them before the cream and dill seed is added.

Orange Sauce for Ham

1 orange (thin peel of orange and fruit
  only—discard white pulp)
$\frac{1}{2}$ pint water
$\frac{1}{4}$ pint sherry
1 tablespoon prepared mustard
2 teaspoons dry mustard

Blend all ingredients for 15 seconds. Pour over ham during the last $\frac{1}{2}$ hour of baking when fat has been removed from drippings in the roasting tin. Baste ham with the sauce from the bottom of the pan several times until done.

Cherry Sauce for Ham

1 (1-pound) tin stoned tart cherries
  (e.g. Morello)
4-ounce brown sugar
2 fluid ounce brandy
2 fluid ounce water
1 tablespoon dry mustard
2 teaspoons cornflour

Drain the cherries and set aside. Blend the cherry juice, sugar, brandy, water and mustard for 10 seconds. Pour over the ham during the last $\frac{1}{2}$ hour of baking, when the fat has been removed from the drippings in the pan.

Baste the ham with sauce from the bottom of the pan several times until it is done. Remove the baked ham to a warm plate. Mix the cornflour with the cherries and then add to the sauce in the roasting pan. Cook and stir over a medium heat until the sauce is clear and thickened. Serve with the ham.

Lamb Kebabs

1 medium onion (quartered)
10 parsley sprigs
1 clove garlic
½ teaspoon peppercorns
2 tablespoons salad oil
1 lemon (peeled)
Salt to taste
1 teaspoon marjoram
1 teaspoon thyme
2-pounds lean boneless lamb (cut into
    1 in. cubes)
Green pepper chunks, red pepper chunks,
    onion chunks, mushrooms brushed
    lightly with oil

Blend onion, parsley, garlic, peppercorns, salad oil, spices and lemon for 30 seconds. Place the prepared lamb in a deep bowl; pour marinade over and marinate for 2-3 hours at room temperature or refrigerate overnight.

Lift lamb from the marinade and string on skewers with green and red pepper chunks, mushrooms and onion chunks. Grill, turning frequently, or use a rotisserie until browned and tender.

Makes 6 servings.

Indian Lamb Skewers

2-pounds lean boneless lamb (cut in
    1½ in. cubes)
2 large onions (sliced)
1 (1-pound) tin apricot halves
1½-ounce brown sugar
3 tablespoons vinegar
2 tablespoons curry powder
1 teaspoon salt
½ clove garlic
Dash cayenne

Blend all ingredients, except lamb, for 15 seconds. Pour into a saucepan and bring to boiling point. Place meat in a large bowl and pour hot mixture over it. Mix well, cover and marinate in the refrigerator overnight.

Thread the meat on skewers or kebab stick, leaving a small space between pieces. Grill or cook on a rotisserie until tender, basting with marinade frequently. Turn meat often to brown evenly. These kebabs are good served with hot cooked rice, sauté courgette slices, a mixed green salad and blender-made ice-cream.

Makes 6 servings.

Grilled Sweet and Sour Spareribs

¼ pint pineapple juice
1-ounce brown sugar
¼ pint wine vinegar
¼ small pepper (sliced)
1 slice onion
1 teaspoon Soy sauce
Salt to taste
3-4-pounds spareribs

Blend all ingredients except the spareribs for 10 seconds. Empty the sauce into a small bowl. Cut ribs in serving portions. Place the ribs in the grill without the rack, and grill under a slow heat for about 20 minutes or until the meat is nearly cooked. Baste with sauce during the last 10 minutes of cooking.

Makes 3-4 servings.

Sauerbratten

No need to chop, chop, chop for the marinade. The blender does it in seconds

¼ pint wine vinegar
2 fluid ounce wine (Rosé or Chianti)
1 onion (sliced)
1 green pepper (coarsely chopped)
1 large carrot (sliced)
4 sticks of celery and leaves (sliced)
8 parsley sprigs
2 bay leaves
1 clove garlic
2 teaspoons marjoram
1 teaspoon peppercorns
1 teaspoon salt
1 teaspoon rosemary
1 teaspoon thyme
1 teaspoon basil
¼ teaspoon ginger
3-4-pounds boneless beef round
4-5 ginger snaps
5 fluid ounce sour cream

Blend all ingredients except meat, ginger snaps and sour cream, for 15 seconds. Place meat in a glass baking dish or a deep bowl and sprinkle lightly with salt and pepper. Pour blended ingredients over the meat. Cover and refrigerate for 48 hours, turning meat at least twice a day. Remove meat from marinade and place in a double roasting tin, or a roasting tin with foil, and pour the marinade over the top. Cover either with the lid of the roasting tin or with tin foil and cook on 300°F/Reg 2 for 3-4 hours or until tender.

Remove meat to a hot plate and keep warm. Crumble ginger snaps into pan drippings. Blend in the sour cream and cook over a low heat, stirring all the time, until smooth. Do not boil. Slice meat and spoon sauce over to serve.

Makes 8 servings.

Sauerbratten

Crown Roast of Lamb with Apple Raisin Stuffing

A dinner spectacular

8-16 rib roast of lamb (tied for crown roast)
Minced lamb (trimmed from the roast)
20 slices of bread (buttered)
4 apples (cored and cubed)
2 eggs
2 onions (coarsely chopped)
4 sticks celery (coarsely chopped)
¼ pint water
6 parsley sprigs
2 tablespoons mint leaves
1½ teaspoons salt
1 clove garlic
6-ounce seedless raisins (soaked in water)

Place the roast on a rack in a shallow roasting tin. Cover the tips of the ribs in tin foil. Roast at 325°F/Reg 3 for 1 hour. Meanwhile prepare the stuffing.

Cook and stir the minced lamb in a frying pan until lightly browned. Drain on paper towels and put in a large bowl. Tear 1 slice of bread into the goblet through the hole in the lid onto the revolving blades. Crumb the remaining bread in the same way, emptying the goblet as necessary. Place in the bowl with the meat. Blend the apples and egg for 20 seconds. Add to the crumbs in the bowl. Blend all the remaining ingredients except the raisins, add to the crumbs along with the raisins and mix well. Remove the partially cooked roast from the oven and pour off all the fat. Mound the stuffing in the centre of the roast. Return to the oven and continue to roast until the meat is cooked (*see* time instructions below). Carefully arrange the roast on a hot plate. Remove the foil from the rib tips and garnish with cherries, paper frills or blanched mushroom caps. Carve between the bones to serve. Plan on 2 rib portions with stuffing per serving.

Roasting time: At 325°F/Reg 3, 20 minutes to every pound (approx.) + 20 minutes.

Makes 4-8 servings.

Grilled Flank Steak Tarragon

2 flank steaks (1-1½-pounds each)
6 tablespoons salad oil
1 large onion (sliced)
6 tablespoons tarragon vinegar
¼ pint Burgundy wine
¼ lemon (thin yellow portion of peel and
   fruit only)
1 teaspoon dry mustard
1 teaspoon salt
2 cloves garlic
1 bay leaf
6 peppercorns

Blend all ingredients except steaks for 20 seconds. Score both sides of steaks in 1 in. diamonds, cutting about ⅛ in. deep. Place steaks in a flat dish. Pour marinade over steaks. Cover and refrigerate several hours, turning steaks several times.

Lift steaks from marinade and grill about 5-10 minutes on each side. Baste with marinade occasionally. To serve, cut in thin diagonal slices.
Makes 4-5 servings.

Marinated Leg of Lamb

1 (5-pound) leg of lamb
¾ pint red wine
3 onions (sliced)
1 carrot (sliced)
¼ lemon (thin outer portion of peel and
   fruit only—discard white portion of
   peel)
1 tablespoon fresh mint leaves
Salt to taste
2 teaspoons oregano
2 cloves garlic
3 parsley sprigs
¼ teaspoon cloves

Blend all ingredients except lamb, for 10 seconds. Place lamb in deep bowl and pour marinade over. Cover and refrigerate for 24 hours, turning meat frequently.

To roast, place meat on rack in shallow baking pan. Roast at 300° F/Reg 2 until ½ hour before the roast is done. Pour off all fat and pour marinade over meat. Cooking time—45 minutes per pound plus 45 minutes.

To serve, remove roast to a warm plate. Heat marinade to boiling, stirring to mix with pan drippings. Serve marinade as sauce.
Makes 8-10 servings.

Blended Beef Hash

½-ounce butter or margarine
6-ounce potatoes (peeled and chopped)
1 small onion (sliced)
6-ounce cooked beef (cubed)
¼ green pepper (cubed)
Salt to taste
4-ounce drippings from the meat
Chili sauce and parsley for garnish

Spread the butter onto deep 9 in. pie plate. With the blender running drop the potatoes and onion through the hole in the lid until chopped. Turn into the pie plate. Do the same with the meat and green pepper. Sprinkle with salt and pour the drippings over. Cover tightly with foil and bake at 400° F/Reg 6 for 20 minutes. Uncover and bake for 10-15 minutes longer or until slightly crisp on top and bottom. Cut wedges to serve and garnish with chilli sauce and parsley.
Makes 2-3 servings.

As an alternative bake the hash as described, only for 20 minutes. Cut the tops from 3 tomatoes, scoop out the insides and fill with hash. Place on a baking sheet and return to the oven for 10-15 minutes.

Spicy Sauced Devilled Eggs

6 hard-boiled eggs
2 tablespoons mayonnaise or salad
  cream
2 teaspoons lemon juice
1 teaspoon dry mustard
1 teaspoon Worcestershire sauce
½ thin slice onion

Peel the eggs and halve them lengthwise. Remove the yolks and blend with all the remaining ingredients, except the egg whites, for 10 seconds. Spoon the yolk mixture into the egg whites. Pour Spicy Tomato Sauce (*see* page 67) into a heat-proof dish and arrange the eggs in the sauce. Cover and place in the oven for 20 minutes at 400° F/Reg 6.
Makes 4 servings.

Tasty Tuna Turnover
Shortcrust Pastry

1-pound plain flour (sieved)
8-ounce lard (or lard and margarine
  mixed)
1 level teaspoon salt
Water to mix

1 small tin condensed mushroom soup
1 large tin tuna (drained and flaked)
½ small onion (sliced)
2 sprigs of parsley
½ teaspoon oregano
¼ teaspoon tarragon

Make the pastry in the traditional way—cut in half and roll each piece out on a lightly floured surface to 8 × 16 in. rectangle. Cut each piece into 8 × 4 × 4 in. squares.
Blend half the tin of soup and all remaining ingredients for 20-30 seconds. The blender may have to be stopped once to push the ingredients back onto the blades.
Place a heaped tablespoon of tuna mixture in the centre of each pastry square. Moisten the edges with water and fold the pastry over to form a triangle. Seal the edges well. Bake at 425° F/Reg 7 for 20 minutes. Serve either hot or cold.
Makes 16 turnovers.

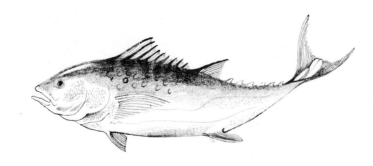

Oyster Cutlets

1 (8-ounce) tin oysters
4 fluid ounce oyster liquor (drained from
  tin)
5 fluid ounce single cream
1-ounce plain flour
1-ounce butter or margarine (softened)
Salt to taste
3 parsley sprigs
Dash of cayenne
2 eggs
Blender-made bread crumbs as required
  (*see* page 8)
Lemon wedges and chopped parsley for
  garnish

Heat oysters in liquor until plump—about 5-8 minutes. Drain, reserving the liquor. Blend the oyster liquor, cream, flour, butter, salt, parsley, cayenne and one egg for 20 seconds. Add oysters and blend for a further 10 seconds. Pour mixture into saucepan and cook, stirring all the time over a medium heat. Cool.
Spoon mixture in mounds on buttered baking tray, using 1 heaped tablespoon per mound to make 8 cutlets. Cover and chill thoroughly. Just before serving whip remaining egg slightly. Dip the patties in egg and then in breadcrumbs. Fry in deep hot fat (350° F) until golden brown, or bake on a buttered baking tray at 350° F/Reg 4 for 30 minutes. Serve with thin lemon wedges and chopped parsley.
Makes 8 patties.

Quiche Lorraine
Shortcrust Pastry

6-ounce plain flour (sieved)
3-ounce fat
Salt to taste
6 teaspoon water

Filling

2-ounce cheese (cubed)
2 slices bacon (cut up)
2 eggs
$\frac{1}{4}$ pint milk
Salt to taste
2-ounce mushrooms
1 medium onion (sliced)

Prepare the shortcrust pastry in the traditional way and line an 8 in. standard flan ring. Prick the base and bake blind for 10-15 minutes at 425°F/ Reg 7.
Place all the ingredients except mushrooms in the goblet and blend for 30 seconds. Stir the mushrooms into the blended cheese mixture before pouring into the partly-cooked flan case and return to the oven for approximately 30 minutes on 350°F/Reg 4 until the filling is set and lightly browned. Serve hot or cold.
Makes 4 servings.

Minute Meat Loaf

1½-pound minced beef ⎱
½-pound minced pork ⎰ in large bowl
4 fluid ounce milk
2-ounce rolled oats
1 egg
1 onion (sliced)
1 stick celery (sliced)
1 clove garlic
4 sprigs of parsley
1 level teaspoon salt
Pepper to season

Place all the ingredients except the meat in the goblet and blend for 20 seconds. Add to meat; mix thoroughly. Place in a lightly greased 2 pound loaf tin. Bake at 350° F/Reg 4 for 1½-2 hours.
Makes 6 servings.

Quiche Lorraine

Spaghetti Bolognaise

1-pound minced beef
¼-pound lean minced pork
2 fluid ounce olive oil
12-ounce tomatoes (quartered) or 1
   medium tin tomatoes
1 beef bouillon cube
¼ pint hot water
1 tin tomato purée
¼ pint dry red or white wine
1 medium onion (sliced)
1 carrot (sliced)
1 celery stalk (sliced)
1 clove garlic
2 bay leaves
1 level teaspoon thyme
1 level teaspoon basil
Hot cooked spaghetti
Parmesan cheese

Cook beef and pork in olive oil in a large heavy based saucepan. Stir constantly until lightly browned and broken up.

Place all the other ingredients except spaghetti and cheese in the blender. Turn on for 30 seconds. Pour into the saucepan with the meat. Simmer for 1 hour stirring often.

Serve over spaghetti and top with grated cheese.
Makes 4-6 servings.

Ham Mousse

8 fluid ounce tomato juice
1 envelope gelatine
1 thin strip lemon peel
1 teaspoon sugar
½ tablespoon chives (chopped)
½ bay leaf
¼ level teaspoon salt
8-ounce cooked ham (cubed)
¼ teaspoon paprika
½ pint double cream
8 ice cubes

Heat tomato juice, gelatine, lemon peel, sugar, chives and salt to boiling point, stirring constantly. Cool slightly. Place ham, paprika and tomato mixture in the goblet and blend for 20 seconds. (The mixture may have to be scraped down during the blending process.)
Once smooth remove the cap and pour in the cream, then the ice cubes whilst the motor is running. Blend for 15 seconds. Pour into a 2 pint mould. Chill. Unmould when completely cold.
Makes 4-6 servings.

Country Chicken

1 (2-3-pound) frying chicken (cut up)
1-ounce plain flour
¼ teaspoon pepper
Salt to taste
1 (1-pound) tin tomatoes
1 medium onion (coarsely chopped)
¼ green pepper (coarsely chopped)
1 teaspoon oregano
¼ teaspoon thyme

Put flour, salt and pepper into a clean polythene or paper bag; add the chicken and shake. Arrange the chicken in a 2 quart casserole. Blend tomatoes, onion, green pepper, thyme and oregano for 10 seconds. Pour over the chicken and bake at 400°F/Reg 6 for 1 hour.
Makes 4 servings.

German Meat Balls

1-pound minced meat
2-ounce blender-made breadcrumbs
Salt to taste
2 fluid ounce milk
1 egg
6 parsley sprigs
¼ teaspoon peppercorns
½ pint water
1 beef stock cube
2-ounce fresh mushrooms
1 medium onion (sliced)
5 fluid ounce sour cream
1 tablespoon plain flour
½-1 teaspoon carraway seeds

Place beef, crumbs and salt into a large bowl. Blend milk, egg, parsley and peppercorns for 5 seconds. Pour over beef and mix thoroughly. Shape into 2 dozen meat balls about 1½ in. in diameter.
Brown balls in a small amount of fat, turning frequently to keep them round. Do one at a time. Blend water, stock cube and onion for 5 seconds. Pour over the meat balls into a saucepan with some of the pan drippings. Simmer for ½ hour. Combine flour, sour cream and carraway seeds. Pour into the saucepan and heat to boiling point, stirring constantly. Lower heat and simmer for 5 minutes.
Makes 4 servings.

Egg Foo Yung

Almost as easy as opening a packet

6 eggs
5-ounce water chestnuts (coarsely
 chopped)
½ green pepper (sliced)
1 stalk celery (sliced)
¼-pound fresh mushrooms or 1 (4-ounce)
 tin mushrooms (drained)
1½-ounce bamboo shoots
Salt to taste
6 peppercorns
4-ounce cubed cooked chicken
1½-ounce butter or margarine

Blend 2 eggs and water chestnuts for 10 seconds. Pour into a large glass bowl. Blend remaining ingredients and remaining eggs, except the butter, for 15 seconds. Add to bowl and mix well. Heat butter in large frying pan. Pour in 2 tablespoons egg mixture for each patty. Fry over medium heat, turning once until lightly browned. Serve with Fugi Sauce (*see* below).
Makes 8 patties.

Baked Stuffed Spareribs

Delicious stuffing and a nice change from barbecued ribs

2-pounds sparerib slabs (2 slabs, boned)
10 slices bread
2 medium onions (coarsely chopped)
2 small apples (cored and coarsely
 chopped)
Salt to taste
1 teaspoon sage
1 teaspoon dry mustard

Place the ribs in a shallow roasting tin. Cover with foil and bake at 350°F/Reg 4 for 1 hour. Crumb the bread, emptying the goblet as necessary and tipping the crumbs into a large mixing bowl. Blend all the remaining ingredients for 10 seconds, add to the bread and mix thoroughly. Remove the meat from the oven; pour off all fat. Mound the stuffing on one slab of ribs. Cover with the second slab and press firmly over the stuffing. Bake for 1½ hours longer or until the ribs are fork tender. If wanted, spoon glaze over ribs ½ hour before cooked.
Makes 4 servings.

Fugi Sauce

Blend ¼ pint water, 1 tablespoon cornflour, 1 tablespoon sugar, 1 tablespoon vinegar and 1 teaspoon dry mustard for 2 seconds. Turn into a saucepan and cook, stirring, for about 5 minutes until clear and thick.

Glaze

Blend 2 oz brown sugar, 2 tablespoons vinegar and ¼ teaspoon ground cloves for 5 seconds.

57

Shrimp Curry

12 oz cooked cubed lamb or chicken may be substituted for the shrimps

1-ounce coconut
¼ pint milk
1 apple (cored and quartered)
1 medium onion (sliced)
¼ pint milk
1-ounce flour
1 tablespoon curry powder
Salt and pepper to taste
⅛ lemon (thin yellow portion of peel and
    fruit only—discard white portion of
    the peel)
8-10-ounce shrimps peeled and de-veined

Infuse the coconut in the milk and pour the mixture through a sieve. Make up to ¼ pint again with water and place the infusion together with all remaining ingredients, except the shrimps, in the blender goblet and blend for 30 seconds.

Pour into a saucepan; add shrimps. Cook and stir over a medium heat until hot and thick, stirring all the time. Lower the heat and cook until the shrimps are hot. Serve over hot cooked rice with a variety of condiments.

Makes 4 servings.

Halibut Creole

½ green pepper (coarsely chopped)
2 stalks celery (sliced)
2 (2 in.) pieces of lemon peel
¼ lemon (peeled)
2 peppercorns
6-ounce fresh or tinned tomatoes (slice
    fresh tomatoes)
1 small onion (sliced)
½ level teaspoon basil
½ level teaspoon oregano
½-pound halibut fresh or frozen (thawed)

Place all the ingredients except the fish in the blender and allow to run for 15 seconds. Pour into

a saucepan, bring to the boil and allow to cook for 5 minutes.

While still hot pour half the sauce into a shallow casserole. Arrange halibut over and cover with remaining sauce.

Bake at 325°F/Reg 3 for 30 minutes or until fish flakes with a fork.

Makes 2 servings.

Baked Stuffed Trout

1 (2-3-pound) trout (cleaned and boned)
    or 2-3 (12-16-ounce) trouts (cleaned
    and boned)
Salt and lemon juice to taste
3 slices bread (buttered)
¼-pound fresh mushrooms (sliced)
1 (2 in.) strip lemon peel
½ stalk celery (sliced)
3 parsley sprigs
1 tablespoon chopped chives
Salt and pepper to taste
Dash nutmeg
Lemon slices and parsley for garnish

Crumb the bread in the blender and put in a large bowl. Chop the mushrooms in the blender and put into the bowl with the bread. Blend all the remaining ingredients except the trout and garnish ingredients for 10 seconds. Add to the bowl and mix thoroughly. Place the fish on buttered foil in a shallow baking tin. Season cavity with salt and lemon juice and fill with the stuffing. Fasten with string. Brush with melted butter. Bake at 400°F/Reg 6 for about 15 minutes per pound. The fish will flake easily with a fork when it is done.

Serve on hot plate garnished with lemon slices and parsley or watercress.

Makes 2-3 servings.

Chicken Fricassée

3 medium leeks or 3 medium onions
1 celery stalk
1 large carrot
4 chicken legs
½ level teaspoon salt
1 clove garlic
5 sprigs parsley
3 fluid ounce cognac
1 level tablespoon plain flour
¼ pint double cream

Wash vegetables, cut in chunks and place in a casserole that has a tight fitting lid. Arrange chicken over vegetables and sprinkle with salt, crushed garlic and parsley.
Pour cognac over. Cover and bake at 325°F/Reg 3 for 1¼ hours or until chicken is tender. Remove chicken to heated plate and keep warm. Pour the rest of the contents of the casserole dish into the blender, add the flour and blend for 15 seconds. Return to the saucepan, cook and stir until thick. Gradually blend in the cream, cook and stir until piping hot. Do not boil. Pour over chicken to serve.
Makes 4-6 servings.

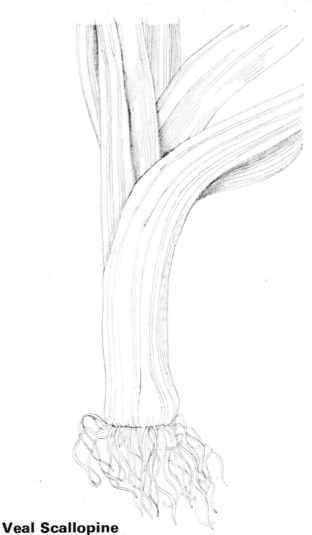

Java Pork Kabobs

2-pounds lean pork (cut into 1 in. cubes)
1 orange (thin outer peel and fruit only
—discard white portion of peel)
1 lemon (thin outer peel and fruit only)
1 small onion (sliced)
2 tablespoons brown sugar
1½ tablespoons Soy sauce
1 tablespoon chili powder
1 clove garlic
¾ teaspoon sugar

Blend all ingredients, except pork, and marinate in the refrigerator for at least 4 hours, stirring several times. String cubes of pork on skewers, leaving small space between each cube. Grill, turning frequently for 15 minutes under medium heat.
Makes 4 servings.

Veal Scallopine

1-pound veal cutlets
Salt, pepper and plain flour as needed
1½-ounce butter or margarine
½-pound mushrooms (sliced)
½ pint dry white wine
1 large onion (sliced)
1 tablespoon sugar
1 parsley sprig
¼ teaspoon rosemary
¼ teaspoon marjoram
¼ teaspoon peppercorns

Season the veal with salt and pepper and dip in flour. Brown quickly in butter. Add mushrooms and set aside. Blend all the remaining ingredients for 5 seconds and pour over the meat in the frying pan. Cover and simmer for 15 minutes or until the meat is tender.
Makes 3 servings.

60

Scrambled Eggs

Cook carefully and slowly for a light lovely texture

6 eggs
3 fluid ounce milk or cream
Salt and pepper to taste
1-ounce butter or margarine

Blend eggs, milk, salt and pepper for 5 seconds. Heat butter in saucepan until hot but not sizzling. Pour in eggs and cook over medium heat. As the eggs begin to set, stir cooked portion away from the sides and bottom of pan and push to the centre. Continue to stir in the same way until mixed and soft but not runny. Remove from heat and serve immediately.
Makes 4 servings.

Ham Scrambled Eggs

Chop 4 ounce cooked ham, passing it through the hole in the centre of the lid onto the turning blades. Place in the pan with the butter and then add the eggs and cook as above.

Cheese Scrambled Eggs

Grate 2 ounce of Cheddar cheese by passing it through the centre of the lid onto the turning blades and sprinkle over the eggs as they cook.

Onion Scrambled Eggs

Chop small sliced onions by passing them through the centre of the lid onto the turning blades and add to the pan with the butter. Add the eggs and cook as above.

Curry Scrambled Eggs

Add $\frac{3}{4}$ teaspoon of curry powder to the eggs before blending them.

Golden Soufflé

2 eggs (separated)
1 small onion (sliced)
1 pinch of salt
$\frac{1}{4}$ teaspoon Worcestershire sauce
4 fluid ounce hot milk
1 ounce butter
2 slices of bread (crusts removed)
4-ounce Cheddar cheese (cubed)

Place egg yolks, onion, salt and Worcestershire sauce in goblet and blend for 10 seconds. Add milk, butter, bread and cheese through the hole in the lid while motor is running. Allow to run until the mixture is smooth.
Whisk the egg whites until very stiff then gently fold the cheese mixture into this. Pour into a lightly buttered 1 pint soufflé dish. Bake at 350° F/Reg 4 for 20-30 minutes. Serve immediately.
Makes 3-4 servings.

Salmon Soufflé

3 eggs (separated)
8 fluid ounce milk
3 slices white bread (crumbed)
1 small onion (coarsely chopped)
1 level teaspoon salt
1 level teaspoon basil
$\frac{1}{8}$ teaspoon thyme
1 (1-pound) tin salmon (drained and flaked)
1 ounce butter or margarine (softened)

Beat egg whites with rotary beater until stiff. Place egg yolks, milk, breadcrumbs, onion, salt, basil and thyme in the goblet and blend for 20 seconds. Add the salmon and butter and re-blend for a further 20 seconds.

Scrape down the sides of the goblet with a spatula and blend again for 30 seconds. Pour salmon mixture over egg white and fold in gently until thoroughly mixed. Turn into a lightly greased 8-inch soufflé dish. Bake at 350°F/Reg 4 for 40-45 minutes. Serve immediately.
Makes 4 servings.

Chinese Egg Rolls

Serve with hot mustard sauce or sweet sauce

8 fluid ounce water
2 eggs
4-ounce plain flour
Salt to taste
½ carrot (coarsely chopped)
½ celery stalk (coarsely chopped)
2 tablespoons bean sprouts
1 onion (sliced)
3-4 ounce cubed cooked meat
1 small tin shrimps (drained)
1 teaspoon sugar
1 teaspoon salt
Dash pepper

Blend water, eggs, flour and salt for 15 seconds. Grease 6 in. frying pan lightly and heat. Pour in just enough batter to make a thin pancake. Bake over a medium heat for 1 minute or until the pancake is firm. Do not turn, remove pancake to a flat surface and allow to cool. Repeat making 8 pancakes and reserving 2 tablespoons batter. Blend carrot, celery, bean sprouts and onion for 10 seconds. Push vegetables to centre of the container and blend for a further 5 seconds. Turn into the mixing bowl. Pour meat through the hole in the lid of the goblet to chop, and add to bowl with vegetables. Do the same to the shrimps before adding to the bowl. Add sugar, salt and pepper and mix thoroughly. Place about 1 tablespoon of shrimp mixture into the centre of each pancake. Roll pancake round filling, fold in ends and seal with reserved batter. Place seam side down on baking sheet and refrigerate for at least 1 hour. Fry in 2 in. hot fat (355°F) until golden brown on both sides. Drain.

Makes 8 egg rolls.

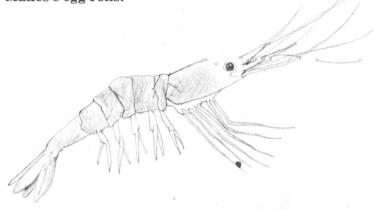

Roast Turkey with Giblet Stuffing

1 (10-12-pound) turkey
1-2-ounce celery leaves
1 teaspoon salt
5 parsley sprigs

20 slices of bread lightly buttered
3 celery stalks (coarsely chopped)
2 medium onions (sliced)
1½-ounce butter or margarine
Cooked giblets (coarsely chopped)
1½ teaspoons salt
10 parsley sprigs
¼ teaspoon sage
¼ teaspoon marjoram
¼ teaspoon rosemary
¼ pint milk

½ pint dripping from roasting turkey
2-ounce plain flour
Salt to taste
1¼ pints stock from cooking giblets

If turkey is frozen thaw it the day before roasting and remove giblets. Simmer in enough water to cover turkey neck and giblets, celery leaves, salt and parsley, until fork tender. Strain liquid and refrigerate. Remove meat from the neck and chop coarsely along with giblets. Refrigerate for use in stuffing.

Tear each slice of bread into half a dozen pieces and with the blender on maximum speed drop the bread through the lid. When the goblet is one third full tip out the crumbs and start again. Empty the crumbs into a large bowl. Chop celery in the same way and tip into a large frying pan. Chop the onion and add this to the frying pan. Add the 1½ ounce butter and cook, stirring over a medium heat for 5 minutes. Place into the bowl with the breadcrumbs. Chop half of the giblets and neck meat, salt and parsley for 10 seconds. Empty into bowl with breadcrumbs. Repeat with the remainder of giblets. Add sage, rosemary, marjoram and milk to the bread and blend thoroughly. Add water, depending on the moistness of the stuffing desired.

Rinse the body and neck cavities of the thawed turkey with cold water. Drain and salt lightly. Pack stuffing lightly into the cavities. Fasten the neck skin with a poultry pin. Fold wings akimbo. Fasten the legs of the turkey and place the stuffed turkey in a shallow roasting pan, breast side up. Brush with melted butter. Cover lightly with tent of aluminium foil and roast at 325°F/Reg 3 for 2½-3 hours. A meat thermometer inserted in the thickest part of the thigh should register 185°F.

Pour or skim fat from the drippings in the roasting pan and then blend the ½ pt of dripping, flour, salt and liquid from the giblets for 5 seconds. Pour into a large saucepan. Cook and stir until the gravy is thick and boiling. Season to taste.
Makes about 16 servings.

Barbecued Chicken

2 fluid ounce water
2 fluid ounce vinegar
1 tablespoon chilli sauce
¼ green pepper (sliced)
1 medium onion (sliced)
1 level teaspoon salt
1 level teaspoon paprika
1 teaspoon Worcestershire sauce
½ level teaspoon dry mustard
1 clove garlic
4 chicken joints

Place all ingredients except the chicken in the goblet and blend for 20 seconds. Arrange chicken in a casserole and pour sauce over. Bake at 375°F/Reg 5 for 1 hour. Serve immediately.
Makes 4 servings.

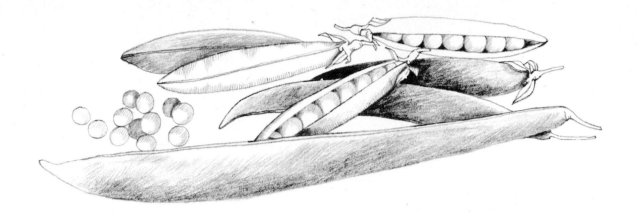

Cheese and Egg Puffs

Sauce

1½-ounce butter or margarine
1 (1-pound) tin of tomatoes
1 medium onion (sliced)
½ green pepper (coarsely chopped)
2 teaspoons plain flour
2 teaspoons sugar
2 (4-ounce) tins sliced mushrooms
  (drained)

Puffs

6 eggs
3-ounce plain flour
1½ teaspoons baking powder
½ teaspoon salt
4-ounce Cheddar cheese (cubed)

Sauce—Heat butter in saucepan. Blend tomatoes, onion, peppers, flour and sugar for 15 seconds. Add to saucepan along with the mushrooms. Cook and stir over a low heat until thick. Simmer for 5 minutes.

Puffs—Sift together flour, baking powder and salt. Grate the cheese by dropping pieces through the hole in the lid whilst the blades are turning. Add the eggs and blend for 30 seconds. Add to the flour and fold in only until blended. Place a couple of tablespoons of batter onto a hot buttered frying pan and bake both sides. Top with sauce.
Makes 4-6 servings.

Chicken Croquettes

2-ounce bread (crumbed)
5 fluid ounce milk or meat stock
1 large onion (sliced)
1½-ounce butter or margarine
1-ounce plain flour
Salt to taste
¼ teaspoon pepper
2 parsley sprigs
12-ounce cooked chicken (cubed)
1 egg (slightly beaten)
2 tablespoons water
Blender-made breadcrumbs as needed

Drop 2 ounce of bread through the hole in the lid of the goblet and put to one side. Blend milk, onion, butter, flour, salt, pepper and parsley for 20 seconds. Pour into a 2 quart saucepan and cook, stirring over a low heat until very thick.
Set aside to cool. Chop the chicken by dropping through the lid hole, and add to the cream sauce. Mix the chicken and cream sauce very thoroughly and leave to chill. Shape the chilled mixture to 8 cones, balls or patties. Chill for several hours. About half an hour before serving time, dip the croquettes in a mixture of egg and water then in the crumbs. Let dry for half an hour. Fry in deep hot fat (375° F). Drain on paper towels. Serve with Spicy Tomato Sauce (*see* page 67), peas or cut green beans in cream sauce or mushroom sauce made by heating tinned mushroom soup.
Makes 8 croquettes.

Lamb Chops Jardinière

6-8 parsley sprigs (chopped in blender)
6 shoulder lamb chops
¾ pint water
3 potatoes (peeled and sliced)
2 leeks (chopped)
1 large onion (sliced)
½ clove garlic (quartered)
Salt to taste
1 teaspoon dry mustard

Brown chops on both sides in a large heavy saucepan. Lift out the chops and pour off the fat. Add water and return chops to the saucepan. Add vegetables and seasonings. Cover and simmer for 30 minutes.

Remove chops to a warm plate and skim off any fat. Pour vegetables and liquid into blender and allow it to cool. Blend for 10 seconds and return to the saucepan with the chops and heat until piping hot. Sprinkle parsley over for garnish.
Makes 6 servings.

Chicken Noodle Casserole

This quick and easy casserole is just right for pot luck and covered dish suppers

8-ounce egg noodles
12-ounce cooked chicken (cubed)
1½-ounce butter or margarine
1 (10½-ounce) tin tomato soup
2 sticks celery (coarsely chopped)
¼ pint rosé wine
½ green pepper (coarsely chopped)
1 onion (coarsely chopped)
Salt to taste
3 parsley sprigs
1 slice of bread torn into pieces
1-ounce Cheddar cheese (cubed)

Cook noodles in boiling salted water according to packet instructions. Drain well and arrange over the bottom of a well buttered 2 quart casserole. Scatter chicken over noodles and dot with butter. Blend soup, celery, wine, green pepper, onion and salt with parsley for 10 seconds. Pour over chicken and noodles.

Drop the bread and cheese through the hole in the lid of the goblet. Sprinkle over the dish. Bake at 350°F/Reg 4 for 30 minutes or until lightly browned and bubbly.
Makes 4-5 servings.

Spanish Pork Tenderloin

4 pork chops (very thinly cut)
2-ounce plain flour ⎤ thoroughly
Shake of salt and pepper ⎦ mixed
1 small tin of mushrooms *or* 4-ounce
  mushrooms (cooked slowly in water
  and liquid retained)
1 small tin of tomato paste
1 small onion (sliced)
½ green pepper (sliced)
1 clove of garlic

Dip the pork chops in seasoned flour. Brown quickly on both sides in a small amount of hot fat. Place in the goblet the liquid from the mushrooms, tomato paste, onion, green pepper and garlic, and blend for 20 seconds. Pour half into a quart casserole. Add the pork and mushrooms then remaining tomato mixture. Cover and bake at 325°F/Reg 3 for 40 minutes. Uncover and continue to bake 20 minutes longer.
Makes 4 servings.

Baked Macaroni Cheese

Rich, full of flavour and ready in no time at all

2 slices white bread (cubed)
½ pint milk
3-ounce Cheddar cheese (cubed)
1-ounce butter or margarine
Salt to taste
3 eggs
2-ounce pimento
¼ green pepper (sliced)
¼ small onion (sliced)
8-ounce macaroni (cooked and drained)

Crumb the bread by dropping cubes through the hole in the lid whilst the blades are turning. Empty into a large bowl. Blend milk, cheese, butter and salt for 20 seconds, adding the eggs through the opening in the lid while the motor is on. Add pimento, green pepper and onion and blend for 5 seconds. Combine with the bread-crumbs and macaroni—mix lightly.

Pour into a buttered 9 × 5 × 3 in. loaf tin and bake at 350° F/Reg 4 for 1 hour or until firm and brown. (You may bake macaroni and cheese in 9 × 13 × 2 in. loaf tin for 45 minutes and then cut into squares to serve.) Cool in the tin for 10 minutes. Turn out onto a warmed plate. Slice and serve with Spicy Tomato Sauce (*see* below).
Makes 8 servings.

Spicy Tomato Sauce

1 (1-pound) tin of tomatoes
1 (6-ounce) tin tomato paste
¼ green pepper (coarsely chopped)
½ small onion (sliced)
1½-ounce butter or margarine (softened)
3 tablespoons plain flour
¼ teaspoon oregano
⅛ teaspoon basil
2 parsley sprigs
¼ teaspoon Worcestershire sauce
Few drops of hot pepper sauce

Blend all the ingredients for 10 seconds and stir over a medium heat until the mixture comes to the boil and is thick.

Ham Timbales

2 slices of bread (buttered)
½-pound cooked ham
¼ pint milk
¼ small onion (sliced)
1 parsley sprig
4 eggs
2 tablespoons sherry
Dash pepper

Crumb the bread by dropping it through the centre hole in the lid, while the blades are turning. Empty into a large bowl. Blend ham, milk, onion and parsley for 20 seconds. Add to the crumbs. Blend the rest of the ingredients for 20 seconds and add to the rest of the ingredients in the bowl. Mix thoroughly.

Fill 6 Dariole or Timbale moulds ⅔ full of the mixture. Set in a pan of water and bake at 350° F/Reg 4 for 25-30 minutes. Cool a few minutes before unmoulding onto a heated plate. Serve with heated mushroom sauce: heat one can of condensed mushroom soup with 2 teaspoons dry mustard.
Makes 3 servings.

Potato Pancakes

Try these topped with apple sauce for a Sunday supper, or serve with Sauerbratten (see page 51)

½-pound potatoes (peeled and cubed)
2 fluid ounce milk
2 eggs
1 slice onion
4 parsley sprigs
Salt to taste
1½-ounce plain flour
¼ teaspoon baking powder

Blend the milk, eggs and onion for 20 seconds, adding approximately ⅓ of the potato through the hole in the lid onto the revolving blades. Add the parsley and another ⅓ potato and blend for 10 seconds. Add the flour and the baking powder and run for a further 20 seconds.

Add the last ⅓ potato through the opening in the lid while the motor is running. Pour 2-3 table-spoons batter into a hot buttered frying pan and fry until brown on both sides.
Makes 8 pancakes.

Sweet and Sour Ham Balls

1-pound cooked ham (cubed)
1 small onion (coarsely chopped)
1 egg
¼ small green pepper (coarsely chopped)
1 level teaspoon dry mustard
2-ounce butter
1 (8-ounce) tin sliced pineapple
1½ fluid ounce vinegar
Cornflour
1 rounded tablespoon brown sugar
1 level teaspoon mustard
½ level teaspoon salt
½ pint water
¾ green pepper (sliced)

Feed the cubes of ham on to the revolving blades through the hole in the lid. (When the goblet is approximately ⅓ full tip the ground ham into a bowl and start again.) Once all the ham has been processed place the egg, onion, ¼ green pepper in the goblet and blend for 15 seconds.

Pour this mixture onto the ham in the bowl and mix well. Form into 12 balls. Heat the butter in a heavy based saucepan, add ham balls and brown on all sides over medium heat, turning often to keep balls round.

Place in goblet the pineapple juice, 3 slices of pineapple, vinegar, cornflour, brown sugar, dry mustard, salt and blend for 15 seconds. Remove ham balls to the heated serving dish. Add the water to the saucepan and stir well to mix in any dripping. Add mixture from blender, whole pineapple slices and green pepper slices. Cook, stirring until the mixture thickens.

Arrange pineapple slices on a plate with the ham balls. Pour over the sauce and garnish with green pepper slices.

Makes 4 servings.

Moulded Chicken Ham Loaf

1 small chicken (cooked)
2 large carrots (cut in chunks)
1 medium onion (sliced)
1 teaspoon salt
2 cloves
4 black peppercorns
12 parsley sprigs
1 envelope gelatine
¼ pint cold water
5 hard-boiled eggs (sliced)
¼ lb cooked ham (sliced)
tomato wedges and parsley for garnish

Strip the cooked meat off the chicken. Boil the bones for 30 minutes in water. Make up to 1 pint and add a chicken stock cube. Add carrots, onion, salt, cloves and peppercorns. Cook until the carrots are tender. Remove the carrots from the broth and chop them with the parsley in the blender for 10 seconds. Put to one side.

Blend cold water, gelatine and hot broth for 40 seconds and put to one side. Oil a 2 lb loaf tin. Arrange egg slices neatly on the bottom of the tin. Alternate layers of egg slices, chicken, parsley, carrot mixture and ham slices. Carefully pour the gelatine mixture from the container over the arrangement in the tin. Cover the tin with foil and press down firmly. The broth should not rise on to the top of the foil. Chill the loaf overnight and unmould by dipping in the warm water and loosening the top edge of the mould with a sharp knife. Invert onto a plate and garnish with tomato wedges and parsley.

Makes 6-8 servings.

Sauces and relishes add zest to a meal. They can turn ordinary left-overs into a memorable feast in a matter of minutes. With the help of the blender all the risk and agony is banished from sauce making. No more ourdled Hollandaise or lumpy white sauce. Just follow the instructions to the last detail and the blender takes care of the rest.

Sauces and Relishes

Speedy Corn Relish and Strawberries with Cardinal Sauce

Tartar Sauce with Scampi

Speedy Corn Relish

2 fluid ounce French dressing
1 tablespoon vinegar
½ pepper (coarsely chopped)
1 stalk celery (sliced)
1 slice onion
2 tablespoons pimento (coarsely chopped)
Salt to taste
1 (1-pound) tin whole kernel corn (drained)

Blend all ingredients except corn for 10 seconds. Pour over the corn and toss to mix. Refrigerate in a covered container for several days so that the flavours can blend.

Cardinal Sauce

1 (10-ounce) packet frozen raspberries (thawed)
4-ounce sugar
1 teaspoon cornflour
1 tablespoon Kirsch (optional)

Blend all ingredients for 40 seconds or until smooth. Strain and chill. Serve over pancakes, strawberries or ice-cream.

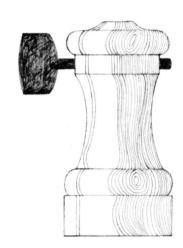

Tartare Sauce

2½ fluid ounce blender mayonnaise
2 tablespoons capers or 6 pimento stuffed green olives (quartered)
6 parsley sprigs
1 slice onion
1 teaspoon prepared horseradish

Blend all ingredients for 15 seconds or until all ingredients are coarsely chopped. Serve with fried, baked, broiled or shell fish.

Fresh Vegetable Sauce

Try this sauce over fish fingers, burgers or cooked vegetables

2 tomatoes (quartered)
$\frac{1}{4}$ green pepper (chopped)
2 slices onion
1 stalk celery (sliced)
6 parsley sprigs
Salt and pepper to taste
$\frac{1}{2}$ teaspoon sugar

Blend all ingredients for 30 seconds. Chill thoroughly.

Steak Sauce

4-ounce carton of cottage cheese
2 tablespoons wine vinegar
1 level teaspoon sugar
$\frac{1}{2}$ level teaspoon dry mustard
1-ounce blue cheese

Place all the ingredients in the goblet and blend for 10-15 seconds. Top with chopped chives.

Mustard Sauce

1 egg
2 fluid ounce water
2 fluid ounce vinegar
2 tablespoons sugar
1 tablespoon dry mustard
$\frac{1}{2}$-ounce butter
Salt to taste

Blend all ingredients for 10 seconds. Cook and stir until thick and smooth.

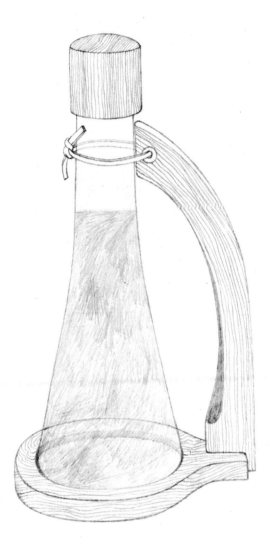

Broccoli Hollandaise

Hollandaise Sauce

2½-ounce butter
3 egg yolks
2 tablespoons lemon juice
Dash of salt and cayenne to taste

Melt butter and heat until just bubbling. Place remaining ingredients in blender, cover and blend for a few seconds. At once pour butter in a steady stream through the hole in the lid. Stop the motor as soon as all the butter has been added.

Mousseline Sauce

Blend ¼ pint double cream and fold into Hollandaise Sauce. Serve with fish.

Bearnaise Sauce

Simmer 3 tablespoons tarragon vinegar, 2 teaspoons chopped onion, 1 teaspoon dried tarragon and pepper to taste until almost all the liquid has gone. Add to Hollandaise Sauce in the blender and blend for 5 seconds. Serve over meats.

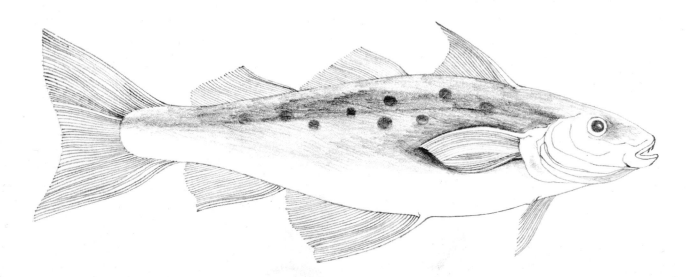

Mocha Sauce

6 ounce Polka Dots
¼ pint hot coffee or ¼ pint hot water and
1 teaspoon instant coffee powder
Small tin evaporated milk

Blend chocolate and coffee for 15 seconds. Add the evaporated milk and blend for another 10 seconds. Serve hot or cold.
You can put 1-2 drops of mint to alter slightly the flavour of this already exciting sauce.

Strawberry and Cranberry Sauce

1 (10-ounce) packet frozen strawberries
or raspberries (thawed)
1 small tin whole cranberry sauce
1 (8-ounce) jar currant jelly

Blend all ingredients for 45 seconds. Strain if desired to remove seeds. Serve over ice-cream, cakes, puddings, fresh fruit. The sauce may be heated if desired.

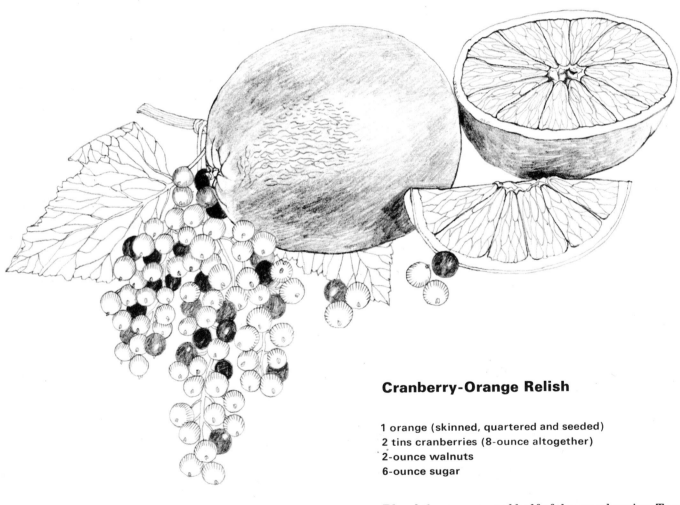

Cranberry-Orange Relish

1 orange (skinned, quartered and seeded)
2 tins cranberries (8-ounce altogether)
2-ounce walnuts
6-ounce sugar

Blend the orange and half of the cranberries. Turn into a bowl. Blend the remaining cranberries and nuts for 15 seconds. Add to the bowl with the sugar and mix well.

White Sauce

A cooking basic, effortless in the blender

½ pint milk or cream
2 tablespoons plain flour
1½-ounce butter or margarine
Salt to taste

Blend all ingredients for 10 seconds. Pour into a saucepan and cook stirring over a medium heat until smooth and thickened.

Horseradish Sauce

Add 3 tablespoons prepared horseradish sauce and ¼ teaspoon sugar.

Tomato Sauce

Add 2-ounce tomato paste.

Parsley Sauce

Add 12 parsley sprigs to the basic white sauce before the ingredients are blended.

Bechamel Sauce

Use ¼ pint of meat or vegetable stock and ¼ pint milk in place of ½ pint milk.

Fresh Cucumber Relish

1 carrot (sliced)
½ onion (sliced)
2 large cucumbers (skinned and cubed)
2 fluid ounce vinegar
Salt to taste
¾ teaspoon dill seed

Blend the carrot and the onion by dropping through the hole in the lid of the blender. Place in a dish to go in the refrigerator. Blend the remaining ingredients for 15 seconds and pour into the dish with the carrot and onion. Chill thoroughly.

Currant-Orange Sauce

½ pint red wine
1 (8-ounce) jar currant jelly
1 orange (peeled, quartered and seeded)
½ lemon (peeled, quartered and seeded)
1 (1 in.) piece of lemon peel

Blend all ingredients for 45 seconds.

Citrus Dressing for Fruit Salad

½-pint pineapple juice
2 eggs
1 1-inch piece lemon peel
2 fluid ounce orange juice
2 fluid ounce lemon juice
2 ounce castor sugar
2 tablespoon plain flour
Salt to taste
½-pint double cream

Blend pineapple juice, eggs, lemon peel, orange and lemon juice, sugar, flour and salt for 15 seconds. Pour into the top of a double boiler or into a bowl over a saucepan of boiling water. Cook and stir over hot water until smooth and thick. Chill. Whip the cream in the blender until it has thickened to a piping consistency. Fold the whipped cream into the dressing.

Cucumber Sauce

Wonderful over salmon or any other fish

1 medium cucumber (peeled and cubed)
2 fluid ounce blender mayonnaise
1 teaspoon lemon juice
Salt and pepper to taste
$\frac{1}{4}$ teaspoon paprika

Blend all ingredients for 30 seconds. Chill thoroughly.

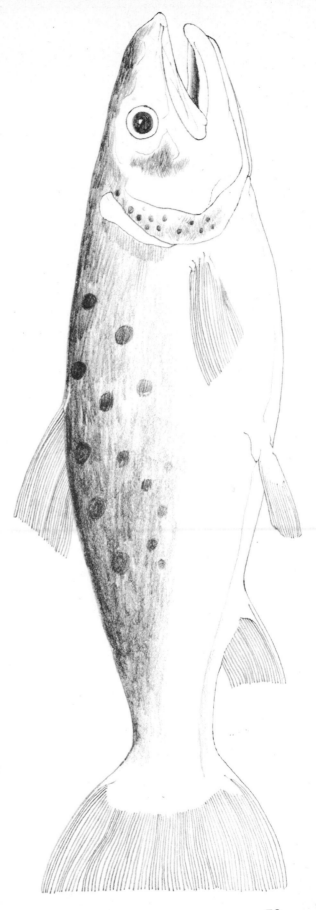

Garden Relish

½ pint tarragon vinegar
6-ounce sugar
Salt to taste
½ teaspoon celery seed
½ teaspoon mustard seed
4-6 ounce sliced cabbage
1 large red pepper (seeded and cubed)
1 large green pepper (seeded and cubed)
1 onion (sliced)
2 carrots (sliced)

Blend vinegar, sugar and seasonings for 10 seconds. Add all the remaining ingredients and blend for a further 10 seconds. Chill in the refrigerator for 24 hours. Pour off excess liquid before serving.

Quick Cheese Sauce

2-ounce Cheddar cheese (cubed)
1 small tin evaporated milk
2 teaspoons Worcestershire sauce
Salt to taste
¼ teaspoon dry mustard

Grate the cheese by dropping it through the hole in the lid whilst the blender is running. Add the milk and seasonings and blend for a further 15 seconds. Pour into a saucepan and cook over a medium heat, stirring constantly until thickened. Serve over vegetables, meats and cooked macaroni or spaghetti.

The recipes in this section are designed to supplement the meat course but they can be served on their own as a lunch or supper dish. If you are tired of boiled cabbage, try the two new ways we suggest—Seven Minute Cabbage with the built-in crunch and Sweet-Sour Cabbage that adds to any pork meal.

Twice Baked Potatoes and Hash Brown potatoes are especially good on a cold winter night, while Tomatoes Provençale give a lift to grilled steaks or chops.

Vegetables

Asparagus Polonaise

Asparagus with Midas Sauce

1 tin asparagus spears or 1-pound fresh
   asparagus (cleaned and trimmed)
¼ pint tomato juice
3-ounce Cheddar cheese (cubed)
1 tablespoon flour
Salt to taste
1 slice bread
½-ounce butter

Cook asparagus in small amount of boiling salt water until just tender. Drain and arrange in a shallow baking dish. Blend the tomato juice, cheese, flour and salt for 15 seconds and pour over asparagus. Butter bread and tear into 5-6 pieces. Crumb it in the blender and scatter over the asparagus. Bake at 375° F/Reg 5 for 15-20 minutes. **Makes 4 servings.**

Vegetables Stuffed Peppers

3 green peppers
1 large tomato (quartered)
1 stalk celery (sliced)
1 slice onion
1 (1-pound) tin whole kernel corn
   (drained)
6-ounce cooked rice
2 slices bread
1-ounce cheese (cubed)

Remove tops and seeds from the peppers. Trim tops from stems and place in blender container. Parboil peppers in boiling salt water for 5 minutes. Drain.
Blend the pepper tops, tomato, celery and onion for 10 seconds, stopping the motor to push the ingredients back onto blades if necessary. Turn into a bowl with the corn and rice and mix. Place the peppers in a baking dish and spoon the vegetable filling in. Tear each slice of bread into 5-6 pieces and crumb it in the blender with the cheese. Sprinkle the crumbs over the peppers and bake at 350° F/Reg 4 for 30 minutes.
Makes three main dish or six vegetable servings. If desired halve the peppers lengthwise, fill and bake.

Hash Brown Potatoes

1-pound potatoes (diced and peeled)
$\frac{1}{4}$ green pepper (coarsely chopped)
16 parsley sprigs
$1\frac{1}{2}$-ounce butter or margarine
Salt to taste
Dash pepper

Chop the potatoes by dropping the cubes through the hole in the lid onto the revolving blades doing about a $\frac{1}{3}$ at a time. Chop the pepper and parsley in the same manner.

Melt the butter in a frying pan and spread the blended ingredients evenly over the bottom of the frying pan. Cover and cook over a low heat for 10-15 minutes. Remove the cover and cook for a further 10-15 minutes or until the bottom is brown and crisp.

Makes 4 servings.

Green Beans Vinaigrette

Garnish with additional chopped pimento and green pepper for a pretty confetti look

1-pound fresh runner beans
3 fluid ounce salad oil
2 fluid ounce vinegar
1 slice onion
$\frac{1}{4}$ small green pepper
$\frac{1}{2}$ tinned pimento
2 tablespoons parsley sprigs
Salt to taste
$\frac{1}{4}$ teaspoon dry mustard

Wash beans and cook in boiling salted water until tender; drain. Blend all ingredients for 15 seconds and pour over beans. Cook over a medium heat until hot.

Chill beans in the Vinaigrette sauce and serve cold as a vegetable for salad.

Makes 4 servings.

Tomatoes Provençale

A wonderful accompaniment to broiled steaks or chops

3 large ripe tomatoes
2 slices bread (toasted)
½ clove garlic
1 onion (sliced)
3 tablespoons olive oil
Salt to taste
Pepper

Halve the tomatoes; place on an oiled baking sheet. Tear each slice of toast into 5-6 pieces and crumb in the blender by dropping through the hole in the lid onto the revolving blades. Pour into a small bowl. Blend the rest of the ingredients for 10 seconds, and pour over the crumbs—toss to mix.

Pile the crumbs onto the tomatoes and cook in a 350°F/Reg 4 oven for 20 minutes or until crisp and hot.

Makes 3 servings.

Scalloped Tomatoes

4 stalks celery (sliced)
2 slices onion (coarsely chopped)
2 tablespoons mustard pickles
2 tablespoons flour
1 tablespoon sugar
Salt to taste
1 (1-pound, 12-ounce) tin tomatoes
3 slices bread (toasted and cubed)

Blend the pickles, celery and onion for 10 seconds, stopping the motor to push the ingredients back onto the blades when necessary. Turn into a 1 quart casserole. Stir in the flour, sugar and salt and then the tomatoes. Crumb the toast in the blender and stir half of the crumbs into the casserole. Bake at 350°F/Reg 4 for 30 minutes. Scatter the remaining crumbs over the top of the casserole and bake 20 minutes longer.

Makes 8 servings.

Tomatoes Provençale

Seven Minute Cabbage

Fresh, tender and delicious! Just remember not to over chop or over cook

1 medium head cabbage (sliced)
2 fluid ounce water
2-ounce butter or margarine
Salt to taste
Dash pepper

Three-quarters fill the blender container with cabbage, add cold water to cover and chop 2-3 seconds—no longer! Drain in strainer or colander. Turn into a saucepan—repeat to chop remaining cabbage. Add all remaining ingredients and heat to boiling. Lower heat, cover and simmer for 7 minutes.
Makes 6 servings.

Sweet-Sour Cabbage

Wonderful old time flavour. Serve in sauce dishes to catch all the good juices

Seven Minute Cabbage (*see* **recipe above**)
3 slices bacon (diced)
2 tablespoons brown sugar
2 tablespoons flour
3 fluid ounce water
3 fluid ounce vinegar
1 slice onion
Salt to taste

Prepare the Seven Minute Cabbage as the recipe directs. Meanwhile cook the bacon until crisp. Drain, reserving 2 tablespoons dripping. Blend the reserved dripping with the rest of the ingredients for 15 seconds. Pour in the frying pan with the bacon, cook and stir until thick. Pour over the Seven Minute Cabbage, mix and serve.
Makes 6 servings.

Courgette Custard

6 medium courgettes (halved)
1½-ounce butter or margarine
3 eggs
8 fluid ounce evaporated milk
1 slice onion
1 whole tinned pimento
½ clove garlic
Salt to taste

Place courgette halves, cut side down in an $11\frac{1}{2} \times 7\frac{1}{2}$ in. baking tin with the butter. Bake at 400° F/ Reg 6 for 15 minutes.

Blend all remaining ingredients for 30 seconds. Pour over courgettes. Place baking tin in larger tin and fill larger tin with water to 1 in. depth and bake at 350° F/Reg 4 for further 40 minutes.

Makes 6 servings.

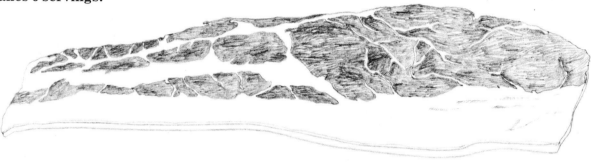

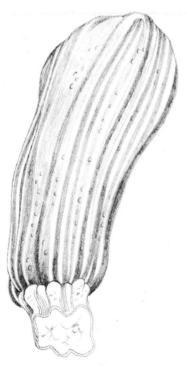

Florentine Spinach

Here's an elegant vegetable perfect for any party dinner

1 (10-ounce) packet frozen spinach
¼ pint sour cream
2 eggs
1 slice onion
1 teaspoon Worcestershire sauce
Salt to taste
Dash pepper

Cook spinach in a small amount of water until tender. Drain. Blend with all other ingredients for 15 seconds. Pour into custard cups or Dariole moulds and place in a pan filled to 1 in. depth with hot water. Bake at 350° F/Reg 4 for 15-20 minutes or until set.

Makes 4 servings.

Twice Baked Potatoes

*Substitute cream cheese for half
the sour cream for extra richness*

6 large potatoes (to be baked)
¼ pint sour cream
1 large onion (sliced)
3 slices bacon (crisp cooked)
Salt to taste

Bake the potatoes at 425°F/Reg 7 for 90 minutes, or until done. Make a crosswise cut in the top, turn peel back and scoop out the potato.

Blend sour cream and all other ingredients with the scooped out potato for 1 minute, stopping motor to push ingredients back onto blades if necessary.

Pile potato mixture into potato shells, sprinkle with paprika. Return to oven for 5-10 minutes.
Makes 6 servings.

Cauliflower Polonaise

*Try Polonaise crumbs over brussel
sprouts, broccoli, cabbage slices,
green beans, asparagus or
boiled potatoes*

1 medium head cauliflower
1 slice bread
1½-ounce butter or margarine
1 hard boiled egg
3 parsley sprigs (optional)

Cook cauliflower in boiling salted water for 10-15 minutes—drain. Toast bread and spread with butter. Cut into 1 in. squares and crumb in blender with egg yolk. Scatter crumbs over cauliflower to serve.

By way of something more traditional, pour a cheese sauce over the cauliflower before adding the crumbs.
Makes 3-4 servings.

Twice Baked Potatoes

Cauliflower with
Quick Cream Sauce

Stuffed Aubergine

2 aubergines (medium)
Salt to taste
½-ounce olive oil or melted butter
2-ounce cooked bacon (diced and
  chopped in blender)
12 sprigs parsley (chopped in blender)
1-ounce mushrooms (chopped in blender)
1 tomato (skinned and chopped)
2-ounce breadcrumbs (crumbed in
  blender)
Salt and pepper to taste
4-ounce cheese (chopped in blender)
1-ounce cheese (chopped in blender)
½ onion (chopped in blender)

Wash the aubergines and remove stalks. Cut in half lengthwise and ¼ inch deep, then lightly score the surface. Sprinkle with salt and brush with olive oil or butter. Place on a greased baking tray in a 400°F/Reg 6 oven until the middle is nearly cooked (approximately 15 minutes).

All ingredients which have to be chopped or crumbed in the blender should be dropped through the hole in the lid onto the revolving blades. Place all remaining ingredients in a bowl (except 1-ounce chopped cheese).

Scoop ⅔ of flesh from the centre of cooked aubergines, place in the bowl and mix thoroughly. Fill the aubergine cases with the stuffing, sprinkle with remaining cheese, and return to the oven for 15 minutes.

Makes 4 servings.

Sauted Carrots with Bacon

3-4 bacon rashers (trimmed)
1 onion (sliced)
1-pound new carrots (scraped and
  sliced)
Salt and pepper to taste
1 teaspoon brown sugar
½ clove garlic
1-ounce butter

Gently fry the bacon over a low heat until crisp. Drain the rashers and set to one side.

Pour the fat into a saucepan. Place the carrots and garlic in the blender and fill with water to just cover. Switch on to maximum speed until the carrots are chopped (4-5 seconds). Tip the contents into a sieve and drain.

Add these carrots to the bacon fat, together with the onion slices, seasoning and sugar, cover the saucepan with a lid and cook over a low heat for 10 minutes. Remove the lid, add the butter and continue cooking until the carrots are slightly browned.

Crumb the crisp bacon in the blender, by dropping it through the hole in the lid onto the revolving blades, and add to the cooked carrots.

Makes 4 servings.

Baked Onions with White Sauce

1-pound medium sized onions (peeled
  but left whole)
½-ounce butter
1 tablespoon water

Sauce

1-ounce butter or margarine
1-ounce plain flour
½-pint milk
Salt and pepper
Sprinkle of mustard powder

Place the onions in a saucepan, cover with cold water and bring to the boil. Simmer for 1 minute. Drain and place in a casserole dish together with the butter and water. Cover and cook in a 350°F/Reg 4 oven for 45-60 minutes or until tender.

Meanwhile, place all the ingredients for the sauce in the blender, switch on to maximum speed and blend for 20-30 seconds. Pour into a saucepan and cook over a low heat, stirring all the time until thick (2-3 minutes).

When the onions are cooked and ready to serve, remove the lid from the casserole, drain off any liquid, and pour the sauce over.

Makes 4 servings.

Children who find a crisp green salad plainly dull can be tempted with such pretty salads as Golden Salad Freeze, Tuna Tomato Aspic and Double Apple Salad.

The Ceylon Chicken Salad is simply delicious and the Green Goddess Salad makes a picturesque centre piece for any buffet supper. There are also eleven variations of the classic French dressings.

Salads and Dressings

Tomato, Aspic,
Ceylon Chicken Salad
and Cabbage Patch Slaw

94

Cabbage Patch Slaw

Choose cabbage with curly outer leaves left on, and reserve these leaves for the cabbage bowl

1-pound sliced cabbage
2 medium carrots (sliced)
½ green pepper (cubed)
1 slice onion
4 parsley sprigs
3 tablespoons vinegar
3 tablespoons sugar
2 tablespoons salad oil
Salt to taste
½ teaspoon dill or celery seed
⅛ teaspoon dry mustard

Three-quarters fill the goblet with cabbage, carrots, green pepper, onion and parsley. Add water to cover and blend for 3-5 seconds or just until the ingredients at the top reach the blades. Drain in a sieve. Repeat with the remaining cabbage. Place in a large mixing bowl. Blend all remaining ingredients for 5 seconds. Combine cabbage and dressing and mix well. Chill before serving.
Makes 8 servings.

Ceylon Chicken Salad

¼ green pepper (cubed)
2 stalks celery (sliced)
12 almonds (blanched)
¾-pound cooked chicken (cubed)
2 tablespoons mayonnaise
2-ounce pineapple titbits (drained)
1 dozen seedless grapes (green)
Salt to taste
1 teaspoon lemon juice

Chop green pepper, celery and almonds by dropping them through the hole in the lid onto the revolving blades. Add to all the remaining ingredients in a mixing bowl and toss to mix thoroughly. Chill. Serve with washed lettuce.
Makes 3-4 servings.

Creamy Tomato Mould

Serve this mould along with cold meat, chicken or shrimp salad

1 envelope gelatine
6 fluid ounce tomato juice (hot)
6 fluid ounce tomato juice (cold)
6-ounce cottage cheese
3 tablespoons mayonnaise
¼ green pepper (cubed)
1 stalk celery (sliced)
1 tablespoon lemon juice
Salt to taste

Blend the gelatine and hot tomato juice for 40 seconds. Add the remaining ingredients and blend for a further 15 seconds. Turn into 4-6 individual moulds and chill until firm. Serve with mayonnaise.
Makes 4-6 servings.

Tomato Aspic

Chill in a ring mould and then un-mould before filling the centre with chilled cooked shrimps, cucumber or potato salad

2 envelopes gelatine
½ pint hot tomato juice
1 bay leaf
3 whole cloves
Salt to taste
1½ pints cold tomato juice
2 stalks celery (sliced)
1 (1 in.) piece of lemon peel
1 lemon (peeled and quartered)

Blend hot tomato juice, gelatine, bay leaf and salt for 1 minute. Add remaining ingredients, except cold tomato juice, and blend for a further 20 seconds. Stir in 1½ pints cold tomato juice. Turn into a 1 quart mould and chill until firm.
Makes 6-8 servings.

Mixed Vegetable Ring

You get lots of fresh vegetable flavour in this nutritious salad

1 envelope gelatine
½ pint hot water
8-ounce cottage cheese
6-ounce carrots (sliced)
4 sticks celery (sliced)
6 parsley sprigs
1 tablespoon lemon juice
Salt to taste

Blend gelatine and hot water for 40 seconds. Add remaining ingredients and blend for a further 15 seconds. Stop motor and push ingredients onto blades if necessary. Turn into a 1 pint mould and chill till firm.
Makes 6 servings.

Avocado Mould

A beautiful salad with pale green colour

1 envelope gelatine
½ pint hot water
1 lime or lemon (thin coloured portion of peel and fruit only)
1 large ripe avocado (peeled, stoned and cubed)
3-ounce cream cheese (cubed)
Salt to taste

Blend gelatine and hot water for 40 seconds. Add remaining ingredients and blend for a further minute or until smooth. Turn into a 1 pint mould and chill until firm.
Serve with tomato slices, strawberries or other fruit.
Makes 6 servings.

Cream and Cheese Mould

This rich salad is perfect topped with fresh, frozen or tinned fruits

1 envelope gelatine
½ pint hot milk
½ pint double cream
6-ounce cream cheese (cubed)
3-ounce Cheddar cheese (cubed)
1 tablespoon lemon juice
Salt to taste

Blend gelatine and milk for 40 seconds. Add all remaining ingredients and blend for a further 20 seconds. Turn into 4 or 6 individual moulds or an 8 in. square tin and chill until firm.
Makes 6 servings,

Cucumber Mould

A perfect salad for a sultry summer day

1 envelope unflavoured gelatine
¼ pint hot water
8-ounce cottage cheese
1 medium cucumber (peeled and cubed)
1 tablespoon mayonnaise
1½-ounce cream cheese (cubed)
2 slices onion
2 stalks celery (sliced)
4 walnuts

Blend the gelatine and hot water for 40 seconds. Add all the remaining ingredients and blend for 30 seconds longer, stopping the motor to push ingredients to blades when necessary. Turn into a pint mould and chill until firm.
Makes 4 servings.

Creamy Vegetable Mould

1 envelope gelatine
8 fluid ounce hot milk
3-ounce cream cheese (cubed)
1½ tablespoons lemon juice
1 teaspoon Dutch or Dijon mustard
Salt to taste
8-ounce sliced red or green cabbage
1 stalk celery (sliced)
6 parsley sprigs

Blend the gelatine and milk for 40 seconds. Add cream cheese, lemon juice, mustard and salt and blend for 10 seconds. Add vegetables and blend for further 5 seconds or until just coarsely chopped. Turn into 6 individual moulds, or a 1 pint mould. Then chill thoroughly.
Makes 6 servings.

Ambrosia

This salad can double as a dessert. Try serving it as an accompaniment to roast duckling

10 dates (stoned)
2-ounce desiccated coconut
1 (1-in.) strip of orange peel
1 (1 in. square) piece candied ginger
3 oranges (peeled and sliced)
1 or 2 bananas (peeled and sliced)
¼-pound seeded black or green grapes

Chop the dates, coconut, orange peel and ginger by dropping them through the hole in the lid onto the revolving blades. Mix with orange and banana slices and black or green grapes, chill thoroughly. Serve on crisp salad leaves.
Makes 4-6 servings.

Green Goddess Salad

6 tablespoons mayonnaise
1 small tin shrimps
2 fluid ounce sour cream
1 hard boiled egg (quartered)
2 tablespoons lemon juice
5-6 parsley sprigs
1 onion (sliced)
1 (4-ounce) tin anchovies (drained)
1 teaspoon Worcestershire sauce
1 clove garlic
½ teaspoon dry mustard
2-3 lettuce
2 (8-ounce) tins shrimps

Blend the mayonnaise, small tin shrimps, sour cream, egg, lemon juice, parsley, onions, anchovies, Worcestershire sauce, garlic and dry mustard for 20 seconds. Pour the dressing over the greens and shrimps in a large salad bowl and toss to coat the greens.
Makes 10 servings.

Ambrosia

Fruited Gelatine

1 envelope gelatine
4 fluid ounce hot water
8 fluid ounce fruit juice (from 15-ounce
  tin fruit)
Fruit from a 15-ounce tin fruit
4-ounce sugar
1 tablespoon lemon juice
Salt to taste

Blend gelatine and hot water for 40 seconds. Add juice, sugar, lemon juice and salt and blend for 10 seconds. Chill until beginning to set, then stir in fruit. Turn into 4-6 individual moulds and chill until firm.
Makes 4-6 servings.

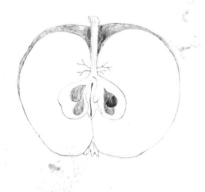

Double Apple Salad

Younger members of the family will want you to add the peanuts

1 envelope gelatine
½ pint hot apple juice
2½-ounce sugar
2 tablespoons lemon juice
2 apples (cored and quartered)
2-ounce roasted peanuts (optional)
¼ teaspoon ginger

Blend the gelatine and hot apple juice for 40 seconds. Add all remaining ingredients and blend for a further 10 seconds. Turn into a 1 pint mould and chill until firm.
Makes 6 servings.

Fast Fruit Slaw

Throw away the grater. You'll never make slaw the old way again

1-pound cabbage (sliced)
1 red apple (cored and quartered)
½-pound grapes (seedless white)
¼-pound pineapple titbits (drained)
¼ pint dairy sour cream
3 tablespoons lemon juice
1 (1 in.) piece lemon peel
2 tablespoons sugar
1 teaspoon prepared mustard
Salt to taste
½ teaspoon celery seed

Three-quarters fill the goblet with cabbage and apple, add water to cover and blend for 3-5 seconds or until the ingredients just reach the top of the blades. Repeat with the remaining cabbage. Drain in sieve then combine with grapes and pineapples. Blend the remaining ingredients for 15 seconds. Pour over the cabbage and toss to mix thoroughly. Chill before serving.
Makes 6-8 servings.

Frosty Pineapple Mould

An extra cool and refreshing salad

1 (13½-ounce) tin crushed pineapple
1 envelope gelatine
1 tablespoon lime concentrate
1 (1 in.) piece of lemon peel
1 medium orange (peeled and quartered)
1 medium cucumber (peeled and sliced)
1 stalk celery (sliced)
Salt to taste
Cucumber slices to garnish

Drain pineapple well, reserving the syrup. Heat the syrup and blend with the gelatine for 40 seconds. Add all the remaining ingredients except the cucumber slices for garnish, blend for a further 5 seconds. Turn into a 1 pint mould and chill until firm.
Makes 4-6 servings.

Red and Green Slaw

¾-pound green cabbage (sliced)
¼-pound red cabbage (sliced)
4 tablespoons mayonnaise
2 fluid ounce sour cream
¾ teaspoon dill seed
Salt to taste
⅛ teaspoon paprika
Dash pepper

Three-quarters fill goblet with cabbage, and add water to cover. Blend for 3-5 seconds or just until ingredients reach the top of the blades. Repeat with the remaining cabbage if necessary. Drain in sieve. Blend all remaining ingredients for 10 seconds. Pour over cabbage and toss to mix. Chill. **Makes 6-8 servings.**

Perfection Salad

An old-fashioned favourite quickly made in your blender. No chopping by hand

1 envelope gelatine
1 tablespoon sugar
Salt to taste
½ pint hot water
4 ice cubes
2-ounce lemon juice
4 stalks celery (sliced)
3-ounce green cabbage (sliced)
1 pimento

Blend gelatine, hot water, salt and sugar for 40 seconds. Add celery, pimento and cabbage and blend for a further 3-5 seconds. Turn into a 1 pint mould and chill until firm.
Makes 6 servings.

Seabreeze Salad

1 envelope gelatine
1 tablespoon lime concentrate
½ pint hot water
¼ pint evaporated milk
1½-ounce cream cheese (cubed)
4 ice cubes
2 tablespoons lemon juice
½ (8¾-ounce) tin crushed pineapple
2-ounce walnuts
Salt to taste

Blend gelatine and water for 40 seconds. Add remaining ingredients and blend for a further 30 seconds. Place in a 1 pint mould and chill until firm.
Makes 4 servings.

Creamy Blue Cheese Dressing

1 (8-ounce) packet cream cheese (cubed)
1 (3-ounce) packet Roquefort or Blue
cheese (cubed)
$\frac{1}{4}$ pint milk
1 tablespoon lemon juice
Salt to taste
$\frac{1}{2}$ clove garlic (optional)
$\frac{1}{2}$ teaspoon tarragon or basil
Dash pepper

Blend all ingredients for 30-40 seconds or until smooth, stopping motor once to push ingredients to blades when necessary.

Cheese Dressing

Serve over assorted greens, fruits and sliced tomatoes

6 tablespoons mayonnaise
2 fluid ounce wine vinegar
3-4-ounce Blue or Roquefort cheese
   (cubed)
1 onion (sliced)
Salt to taste
$\frac{1}{4}$ teaspoon paprika
$\frac{1}{8}$ teaspoon dry mustard
Dash pepper

Blend all ingredients for 20 seconds.

Sunny Carrot Salad

1-pound carrots (sliced)
12-ounce pineapple chunks (drained)
3-ounce seedless raisins
4 tablespoons mayonnaise
Salt to taste
¼ teaspoon nutmeg

Place the carrots in the blender and cover with water. Blend for 2-3 seconds or just until carrots on top reach the blades. Drain in sieve. Add remaining ingredients and toss thoroughly to mix.
Makes 6 servings.

Hot Potato Salad

Perfect for a patio or a barbecue supper

6 medium potatoes
4 slices bacon (diced)
3 fluid ounce cider vinegar
2 slices onion
2 stalks celery (sliced)
6 parsley sprigs
1-2 tablespoons sugar
Salt to taste
¼ teaspoon marjoram or basil

Cook potatoes in boiling salted water until tender. Drain, and keep warm. Cook bacon in frying pan until crisp. Place vinegar, onion, celery and parsley in the blender and switch on for 2-3 seconds. Add to the bacon and fat in the frying pan and heat to boiling. Cube or slice the potatoes into a bowl and pour the bacon mixture over the top. Toss lightly to mix. Serve hot.
Makes 4 servings.

Lemon Salad Dressing

2 pieces lemon peel
1 lemon (peeled)
4 fluid ounce water
1 level teaspoon dry mustard
½ level teaspoon pepper
½ small onion (sliced)
¼ level teaspoon paprika

Take the lemon peel off with a potato peeler to get a very thin piece without the pith. Place all the ingredients in the goblet and blend for 15 seconds.
Serve on a green salad.

Above, Sunny Carrot Salad
Left, Creamy Blue Cheese Dressing

Golden Salad Freeze

1 (8-ounce) tin apricot halves
2 packets gelatine
2 tablespoons lemon juice
1 (1-pound, 13-ounce) tin fruit
   cocktail
½ pint double cream
6-ounce cream cheese (cubed)
½ lemon (thin portion of peel and fruit
   only)
2 tablespoons mayonnaise
12 marshmallows (quartered)
6 maraschino cherries (halved)

Drain apricots reserving the syrup. Make the syrup up to ½ pint, heat and then blend the syrup and gelatine for 40 seconds. Add the apricots and blend for a further 10 seconds. Pour into a large bowl.

Drain the fruit cocktail reserving the syrup, and place the syrup in the goblet along with the cream cheese, lemon and mayonnaise. Blend for 20 seconds. Pour into the large bowl with the first blend. Add the fruit cocktail, marshmallows and cherries and place into decorative moulds after the ingredients in the bowl have been very thoroughly mixed.

Unmould once the mixture has been chilled until set, and let it stand at room temperature for about 5 minutes before cutting if it is in a larger mould.
Makes 8-10 servings.

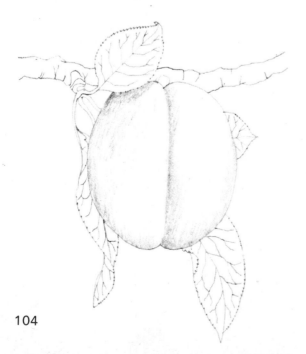

Scandinavian Cucumbers

A summertime favourite

¼ pint sour cream
2 tablespoons tarragon vinegar
2 tablespoons sugar
6 parsley sprigs
1 slice onion
½ teaspoon dill seed
2 medium cucumbers (sliced)

Blend sour cream, vinegar, sugar, parsley, onion and dill seed for 10 seconds. Pour over cucumbers and chill thoroughly.
Makes 6 servings.

Vegetables Basket Salad

Cottage cheese ring mould holds tangy marinated vegetables. Add hot rolls, a beverage and a dessert and you have a luncheon

2 (1-pound) tins mixed vegetables
¼ pint French dressing (*see* page 106)
Packet gelatine
¼ pint hot water
12-ounce cottage cheese
12 fluid ounce mayonnaise
¼ pint cream
6 parsley sprigs
1 whole pimento
1 slice onion
1 tablespoon lemon juice
Salt to taste
½ teaspoon Worcestershire sauce

Drain the vegetables and pour the French Dressing over and chill whilst preparing the rest of the salad. Blend the gelatine and hot water for 40 seconds. Add all the remaining ingredients and blend for a further 15 seconds. Turn into a 1½ pint mould and chill until firm. Unmould onto a serving plate and fill the centre with the marinated vegetables.
Makes 8 servings.

Tuna Tomato Aspic

Chill this pretty red salad in a fish mould

1 envelope gelatine
1 tablespoon sugar
Salt to taste
Dash hot pepper sauce
½ pint water (hot)
8-9 ice cubes
2 (8-ounce) tins tomato sauce
2 (7-ounce) tins tuna

Blend the gelatine, sugar, salt, hot pepper sauce and hot water for 40 seconds. Add the ice cubes and tomato sauce and blend for further 30 seconds. Drain and flake the tuna. Add to the gelatine mixture and turn into a 1½ pint mould allowing to chill and firm.
Makes 8 servings.

Salmon Coleslaw

1-pound sliced cabbage
1 (1-pound) tin salmon
4 tablespoons mayonnaise
1 rounded tablespoon capers

Three-quarters fill the blender with the cabbage, add water to cover. Blend for 3-5 seconds or just until the cabbage at the top reaches the blades. Drain in a sieve. Repeat with the remaining cabbage if necessary. Drain and flake the salmon, add to cabbage along with the mayonnaise and capers. Toss thoroughly to mix. Chill before serving.
Makes 6 servings.

Caesar Salad

One of the salad greats, updated for the blender. Serve Caesar Salad as a first course on chilled dinner plates

2 slices day-old bread (crumbed)
2 tablespoons salad oil
1 egg
2 tablespoons salad oil
3 tablespoons lemon juice
½-ounce Parmesan cheese
4 anchovy fillets (optional)
½ clove garlic
Salt to taste
4 peppercorns or ½ teaspoon pepper
1 large head of lettuce

Sauté breadcrumbs in 2 tablespoons oil until lightly browned. Blend all the remaining ingredients, except the lettuce, for 15 seconds. Pour the dressing over the lettuce and toasted bread cubes.
Makes 4 servings.

Potato Salad

Garnish with sliced tomatoes and cucumbers for pretty colour

4 celery stalks (sliced)
1 small onion (coarsely chopped)
2 tablespoons parsley sprigs
1-pound potatoes (cooked and cubed)
Salt to taste
Mustard salad dressing (*see* page 107)

Drop the celery, onion and parsley through the hole in the lid of the goblet onto the revolving blades. Add to the potatoes in a large mixing bowl along with salt and mustard dressing. Toss to mix well and chill thoroughly.
Makes 6-8 servings.

French Dressing

Once you try this you will make lots of your own variations. You'll probably develop your own speciality of the house

½ pint oil
3 tablespoons lemon juice or vinegar
1 slice onion
1 tablespoon sugar
2 teaspoons paprika
Salt to taste

Blend all ingredients for 20 seconds in the blender.

Garlic Dressing

Add 1-2 cloves garlic before blending.

Classic French Dressing

Add 4 peppercorns, ¼-½ teaspoon dry mustard before blending.

Avocado Dressing

Peel, stone and cube 1 ripe avocado and add before blending.

Citrus Dressing

Peel and quarter 1 orange and add before blending.

Parsley French Dressing

Add 1 dozen parsley sprigs and ½ teaspoon celery seed before blending.

Tomato French Dressing

Add 1 quartered tomato and ½ teaspoon celery seed before blending.

Creamy French Dressing

Add 2 tablespoons mayonnaise and 1 teaspoon tomato ketchup before blending.

Lorenzo Dressing

Add ½ ounce watercress tops, 3 tablespoons chilli sauce and 1 onion (slice before blending).

Celery Seed

Add 1 teaspoon celery seed before blending.

Dilly Dressing

Add 1 teaspoon dried dill or ½ teaspoon dill seed before blending.

Piccalilli Dressing

Add 2 sweet or 1 dill pickle sliced and 1 pimento before blending.

Blender Mayonnaise

Easy to make and perfect every time

1 egg or 2 egg yolks
2 tablespoons lemon juice or vinegar
½ teaspoon sugar
½ teaspoon salt
¼ teaspoon dry mustard
¼ pint salad oil

Blend egg, lemon juice, salt, pepper, mustard for 60 seconds adding the oil in a steady stream through the hole in the lid while the motor is running.

Banana Mayonnaise

Add 1 banana peeled and quartered and blend for 5-10 seconds longer.

Pineapple Mayonnaise

Add 2 slices drained tinned pineapple to mayonnaise and blend for 5-10 seconds longer.

Honey of a Dressing

Wonderful over fresh or tinned fruit in a salad

4-ounce honey
2 tablespoons olive oil
2 tablespoons lemon juice
2 fluid ounce water
¼ teaspoon ginger
Salt to taste

Blend all ingredients for 30 seconds in the blender.

Cooked Salad Dressing

2 eggs
6 fluid ounce water
3 fluid ounce vinegar
2-ounce sugar
1 tablespoon plain flour
2 teaspoons dry mustard
Salt to taste

Blend all ingredients for 20 seconds, and pour into a double saucepan or bowl over a saucepan which contains boiling water. Cook and stir over the hot water until smooth and thick. Cool, then cover and chill.

Tarragon Lemon Dressing

Add a few tablespoons of this dressing to chicken salad

½ pint salad oil
2 (1 in.) pieces of lemon peel
1 whole lemon (peeled)
2 tablespoons tarragon vinegar
½ tablespoon sugar
1 teaspoon tarragon
½ teaspoon salt
6 peppercorns

Blend all ingredients for 40 seconds in the blender.

Mustard Salad Dressing

Great for potato salad or tuna salad

1 rounded tablespoon prepared mustard
2 tablespoons cream or evaporated milk
2 tablespoons sugar
2 tablespoons cider vinegar
Salt and pepper to taste

Blend all ingredients for 20 seconds in the blender.

Frozen Roquefort Dressing

Cut small cubes of this dressing to scatter over fruit salads or melon wedges

$\frac{1}{4}$ pint cream
2 tablespoons mayonnaise
3-ounce cream cheese (cubed)
3-4-ounce Roquefort or Blue cheese
1 (1-in.) piece of lemon peel
1 whole lemon (peeled)
2 stalks celery (sliced)
Salt to taste

Blend all ingredients for 40 seconds. Pour into an 8 in. square pan or ice cube container and freeze firm. Cut into cubes.

Creamy Cucumber Dressing

3 fluid ounce sour cream
$\frac{1}{4}$ medium cucumber (peeled and sliced)
1$\frac{1}{2}$ tablespoons vinegar
2 teaspoons sugar
1 slice onion
$\frac{3}{4}$ teaspoon salt
$\frac{1}{8}$ teaspoon dry mustard
$\frac{1}{8}$ teaspoon pepper

Blend all ingredients in the blender for 20 seconds.

Confetti Dressing

6 fluid ounce salad oil
3 tablespoons wine vinegar
2 tablespoons lemon juice
1 small cooked beetroot (sliced)
1 hard boiled egg
6 parsley sprigs
1 teaspoon sugar
1 teaspoon salt
1 teaspoon paprika
$\frac{1}{2}$ teaspoon dry mustard

Blend all ingredients for 10 seconds in the blender.

Brandy Dressing

2 fluid ounce salad or olive oil
2 fluid ounce brandy
2 teaspoons sugar
$\frac{1}{2}$ teaspoon nutmeg

Blend all ingredients in the blender.

With the use of your blender ice cream making becomes a real joy. If you follow the Vanilla Custard Ice-Cream and use this as your basic recipe all kinds of fruit can be added. Home-made ice-cream can be expensive but we have deliberately chosen recipes—using evaporated milk for instance—suitable for normal family life. Lemon Ice, Orange Divine are two money savers that the family will love. Try the Chocolate Dessert Pancakes which can be made in advance and kept warm in the oven, and delicacies like Strawberry Bavarian Cream, Apricot Custard and Pineapple Cream. One last plea: don't miss the Chocolate Angel Pie—it really is food for the angels.

Desserts

1 Orange Pistachio Parfait
2 Ginger Cream
3 Ice-Cream with Strawberry and
    Cranberry Sauce
4 Chocolate Angel Pie
5 Apricot Chiffon Pie

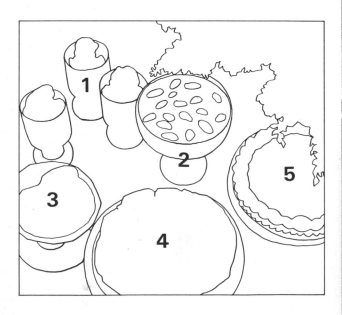

Chocolate Angel Pie

Angel Pie Shell

3 egg whites
Pinch of salt
$\frac{1}{8}$ teaspoon cream of tartar
6-ounce castor sugar
4-ounce blanched almonds
1 teaspoon almond essence

Filling

4-ounce chocolate (plain)
3 tablespoons hot strong coffee
1 tablespoon cognac
$\frac{1}{4}$ pint double cream

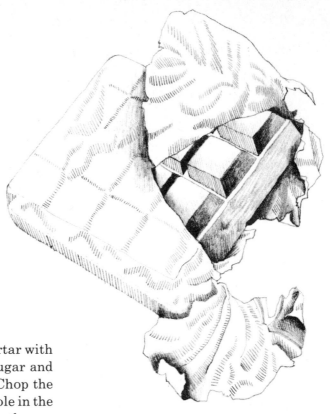

Angel Pie Shell

Beat the egg whites, salt and cream of tartar with whisk until foamy. Gradually add the sugar and beat it until the mixture is really stiff. Chop the almonds by dropping them through the hole in the lid whilst the blades are revolving. Add to the egg whites along with the almond essence. Fold together until the nuts are evenly distributed. Spread over the bottom and up the sides of the 9 in. plate or dish and bake at 350°F/Reg 4 for 45 minutes or until lightly browned. Cool completely.

Filling

Break the chocolate into squares and drop through the hole in the lid onto the revolving blades. Add the coffee and blend for a further 30 seconds. Add cognac and blend for 5 seconds. Pour over the whipped cream and mix together until blended. Pour into cooled pie shell. Chill for at least 3 hours.
Makes 6-8 servings.

Ginger Cream

2-ounce blanched almonds
4 fluid ounce milk (hot)
8-ounce white marshmallows (quartered)
2 fluid ounce cold milk
1 envelope gelatine
2-ounce crystallised ginger
2 tablespoons rum
$\frac{1}{4}$ pint double cream

Chop the almonds by dropping them through the hole in the lid onto the revolving blades. Place hot milk, marshmallows, cold milk, gelatine and ginger in the goblet and blend for 30 seconds. If the marshmallows have not melted continue to blend. Leave in the goblet until the mixture just begins to set. Re-blend and add the rum and cream by pouring onto the revolving blades. Pour into mould and chill until firm.
Makes 4 servings.

Apricot Chiffon Pie

Try this delicious apricot filling in a Ginger Crumb Crust (see page 120).
The addition of cracked ice helps the filling to set more quickly.

2 eggs (separated)
2 tablespoons castor sugar
1 packet gelatine
4-ounce dried apricots
¼ pint orange juice concentrate
¼ pint hot milk
1½-ounce castor sugar
¼ pint double cream
½ tray ice cubes
1 (9 in.) baked pastry shell

Beat the egg whites until soft peaks form. Gradually add the 2 tablespoons sugar and continue beating until stiff. Blend the gelatine, apricots, orange juice concentrate and hot milk for 40 seconds. Add sugar and egg yolks and blend for 15 seconds. Add the cream and blend for 40 seconds, gradually adding the ice through the hole in the lid whilst the motor is running. Fold the apricot mixture into the egg whites until smooth. Pile in a pastry shell and chill until firm.
Makes 6 servings.

Orange Pistachio Parfait

2-ounce blanched pistachios
1 small orange (pared-off peel and fruit)
½ lemon (pared-off peel and fruit)
3-ounce castor sugar
4 fluid ounce water
3 eggs
2 tablespoons cold water
1 envelope gelatine
¼ pint double cream

Chop the nuts by dropping them on to the revolving blades. Empty into bowl. Blend together orange, lemon, sugar and water for 20 seconds. Pour into saucepan and bring to the boil. Place eggs, cold water and gelatine in the goblet and blend for 20 seconds, adding the hot mixture through the opening in the lid whilst the motor is running. Empty back into saucepan, cook and stir over low heat until slightly thickened. Pour into ice tray and freeze until mushy. Return to the blender, add cream and nuts (reserving a tablespoonful for decoration) and blend for 25 seconds. Return to ice trays or sherbet dishes and re-freeze. Decorate with nuts.
Makes 4 servings.

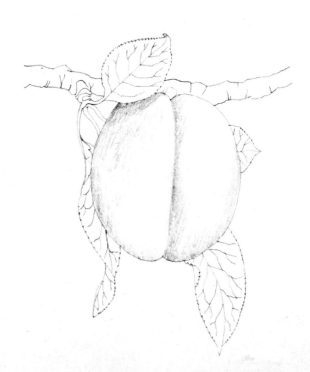

Vanilla Custard Ice-Cream

¼ pint double cream ⎱ mixed together
½ pint single cream ⎰
1½-ounce castor sugar
1 tablespoon flour
½ teaspoon vanilla essence

Blend half the cream and the rest of the ingredients together for 20 seconds. Pour into a saucepan and stir over a medium heat until thickened. Cook 2 minutes longer. Put into the goblet and add remaining cream and vanilla through the hole in the lid. Pour into the ice tray and freeze. When slushy remove from tray and re-blend for 10 seconds. Return to freezer.
Makes 6 servings.

Strawberry Ice-Cream

Blend together ½-pound strawberries and 1-ounce sugar until smooth. Stir into partially frozen ice-cream and continue freezing.

Banana Ice-Cream

Blend 1 banana (peeled and sliced) with ½ lemon (peeled) for 20 seconds. Add to chilled ice-cream before freezing.

Orange Divine

5 fluid ounce boiling water
2 envelopes gelatine
2-ounce castor sugar
1 tin (large) frozen orange concentrate
1 tray ice cubes

Blend water, gelatine and sugar together for 15 seconds. Add orange and ice and blend for a further 45 seconds. Let this stand for 1-2 minutes. Spoon into serving dishes.
Makes 4 servings.

Strawberry Ice-Cream

1 large tin evaporated milk
1-ounce castor sugar
4 fluid ounce water
2 level tablespoons cornflour
10-ounce frozen strawberries (partially thawed) or fresh ripe strawberries

Place half the evaporated milk in the freezer compartment and allow to become very cold. Into the goblet put the rest of the milk, sugar, water and cornflour and blend for 10 seconds. Transfer to a saucepan, bring to the boil and cook for 2 minutes stirring all the time. Chill thoroughly. Place the cold evaporated milk in the goblet and blend for 30 seconds until it begins to thicken. Add the thickened mixture and strawberries and blend until it is smooth. Freeze until firm. Decorate with whipped cream flavoured with crème de menthe.
Makes 6 servings.

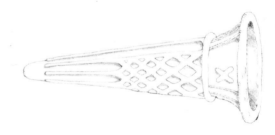

Chocolate Freeze

1-ounce castor sugar
4 fluid ounce water
6-ounce mint flavoured chocolate
3 egg yolks
¼ pint double cream

Boil the sugar and water for 3 minutes. Place in goblet with the chocolate and blend until the chocolate is melted. Add egg yolks and re-blend for 10 seconds. Cool to room temperature. Add cream by pouring in through the hole in the lid. Arrange in 8 small dishes, cover and freeze until firm. Decorate with fresh cream.
To make this extra specially good, use 'After Eight Mints'.
Makes 4 servings.

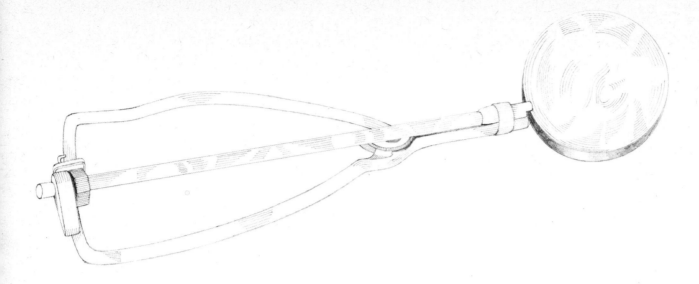

Lemon Ice

4-ounce castor sugar
8 fluid ounce water
1 lemon (pared-off peel and fruit)
1 large piece of crystallised ginger
Few drops of yellow colouring

Boil sugar and water for 5 minutes. Remove from heat. Place lemon peel, fruit and ginger in the goblet and blend for 10 seconds. Gradually add the hot sugar syrup through the hole in the lid while the motor is running. Add food colouring as required.

Pour into an ice tray and freeze until slightly firm (approx. 2 hours). Scrape from the tray and re-blend for 20 seconds. Return to the ice tray and freeze until firm.

Makes 4 servings.

Banana Glacé

1 egg white
4-ounce castor sugar
2 bananas (peeled and sliced)
2 fluid ounce cognac
½ pint single cream

Beat the egg white with rotary whisk until foamy. Gradually add 2 tablespoons sugar and continue beating until stiff. Place bananas, remaining sugar and cognac in the blender goblet and allow to run for 15 seconds. Add the cream through the hole in the lid and continue to blend until the mixture is smooth.

Pour into the bowl containing the egg white mixture. Fold in until thoroughly blended. Pour into ice tray and freeze until firm.

Makes 4 servings.

Vanilla Sauce

4 egg yolks
2½-ounce castor sugar
1 teaspoon cornflour
Pinch of salt
¾ pint milk
1 teaspoon vanilla essence
4-ounce double cream (optional)

Blend egg yolks, sugar, cornflour and salt for 30 seconds. Add the milk and blend for a further 10 seconds. Pour into saucepan. Cook and stir over low heat until the mixture is thickened and coats the metal spoon. Stir in vanilla, cool, stirring occasionally.
For an extra rich sauce return the cool sauce to the blender and add the double cream through the opening in the lid. Serve over fruit.

Lemon Sauce

1 lemon (thin yellow portion of peel and
   fruit only)
½ pint boiling water
1 egg
4-ounce castor sugar
2 fluid ounce cold water
2 tablespoons cornflour
½-ounce butter or margarine
Salt to taste
⅛ teaspoon nutmeg

Blend all ingredients for 10 seconds. Pour into a saucepan and cook and stir until smooth and thick. Serve over Lemon Pudding (see page 122).

Hard Sauce

Delicious over mince pies or plum pudding

2-ounce butter (softened)
2 tablespoons brandy
6-ounce icing sugar (sieved)

Blend all ingredients together for 20 seconds or until smooth.

Thin Hard Sauce

8 fluid ounce boiling water
5-ounce castor sugar
¼ lemon (pared-off peel and fruit only)
1-ounce butter
1 tablespoon cornflour
1 tablespoon brandy

Place all ingredients in the goblet except the brandy and blend for 10 seconds. Pour into saucepan and cook over low heat, stirring all the time until thick and clear. Add brandy.

Chocolate Chiffon Pie

1 large tin evaporated milk (chilled icy
   cold)
1 packet gelatine
5-ounce castor sugar
Salt to taste
1 egg yolk
6 fluid ounce milk
3-ounce plain chocolate (broken into
   squares)
1 teaspoon vanilla or peppermint
   essence
1 (9 in.) baked pastry shell

Whisk the evaporated milk until stiff. Empty
into a bowl and chill while preparing the filling.
Blend all remaining ingredients except vanilla
and pastry shell for 20 seconds. Empty into a
saucepan and stir over a medium heat just until
the mixture begins to steam. Do not boil. Cool
slightly, return to the container and blend for
40 seconds or until smooth.
Pour into a bowl and chill until the mixture
mounds when spooned. Fold in the whipped milk
and vanilla. Turn into baked pastry shell and
chill until firm. Decorate with whipped cream.
Makes 6 servings.

Strawberry Bavarian Cream

2 fluid ounce cold milk
1 packet gelatine
1-ounce castor sugar
1 (10-ounce) package frozen strawberries
   (thawed)
2 egg yolks
½ tray of ice cubes
¼ pint double cream

Heat the milk to simmering and then place in the
goblet with the gelatine. Blend for 15 seconds.
Add the sugar, strawberries and egg yolks—
blend for a further 30 seconds.
Feed the ice and cream onto the revolving blades
through the hole in the lid. Turn into a 1 pint
mould and chill.
Makes 4 servings.

Orange Cheese Cake

6-ounce Marie biscuits
2 tablespoons castor sugar
2½-ounce butter or margarine (melted)
½-pound cottage cheese
4 fluid ounce milk
2 eggs
¼ small orange (pared-off peel and fruit)
1-ounce castor sugar
1 tablespoon flour

Crumb the Marie biscuits by dropping them onto
the revolving blades. Empty into a mixing bowl,
add the sugar and stir in the melted butter. Press
three-quarters of the crumbs into a lightly greased
8 in. pie dish or flan ring. Chill.
Place the rest of the ingredients in the goblet and
blend for 40 seconds. Pour into crumb-lined dish,
sprinkle with reserved crumbs. Bake at 325°F/
Reg 3 for 1 hour, or until the cheese cake is firm.
Chill.
Makes 6 servings.

Whipped Cream

Whip ½ pint cream for 60-90 seconds, stopping
the motor at 20 second intervals to see if the cream
is sufficiently whipped. If desired add 1-2 tablespoons castor sugar and ½ teaspoon vanilla
essence during the last 10 seconds of whipping.
Use in recipes calling for whipped cream, or for
decoration.

Cherry Pie

8-ounce digestive biscuits
3-ounce butter (melted)

1 tin cherries (stoned)
1 level tablespoon arrowroot
$\frac{1}{4}$ teaspoon almond essence

Crumb the biscuits by dropping pieces through the hole in the lid onto the revolving blades. Transfer the crumbs into a saucepan containing the butter, and mix until the crumbs are moist. Press into either an 8 in. flan ring or pie dish. Leave to one side to set.

Place the cherry juice, arrowroot and almond essence in the goblet and blend for 10 seconds. Transfer to a saucepan, bring to the boil and cook for 2 minutes stirring all the time. Add the cherries—pour into the pie crust.

Chill thoroughly before serving. Serve with cream.

Makes 6 servings.

Nesselrode Chiffon Pie

As a variation, serve this in individual sundae dishes

2-ounce maraschino cherries (well drained)
1-ounce walnuts
$1\frac{1}{2}$-ounce plain chocolate
1 packet gelatine
2 fluid ounce cold milk
3 egg yolks
2-ounce castor sugar
Salt to taste
6 fluid ounce milk (hot)
3 egg whites
2-ounce castor sugar
3 tablespoons sherry or rum
$\frac{1}{4}$ pint double cream (whipped)
1 (9 in.) baked pastry shell
Grated chocolate and maraschino cherries for decoration

Chop the cherries by dropping them through the hole in the lid onto the revolving blades. Chop the chocolate and walnuts in the same way and add them to the cherries.

Blend the gelatine and cold milk for 10 seconds. Add egg yolks, 2 ounce sugar and salt and blend for a further 30 seconds, adding the hot milk through the hole in the lid while the motor is running. Pour into a bowl and chill until the mixture mounds when spooned.

Beat the egg whites until foamy. Gradually add 2-ounce sugar and continue to beat into stiff peaks. Add sherry to the gelatine mixture and pour over the egg whites. Add the cherries, nuts and chocolate and whipped cream and fold together until smooth. Pile into pastry shell. Chill until firm. Decorate with grated chocolate and cherries.

Makes 6 servings.

Almond Stuffed Apples

4-ounce blanched almonds
1 tablespoon water
2-ounce castor sugar
$\frac{1}{4}$ teaspoon almond essence
4 medium baking apples
Melted butter or margarine
Blender breadcrumbs
Castor sugar
$\frac{1}{4}$ pint double cream (whipped)

Chop the almonds by dropping them through the hole in the lid onto the revolving blades. Empty onto a piece of waxed paper. Blend the water. sugar and almond essence for 10 seconds. Add the ground almonds and blend for a further 40 seconds, stopping the motor when necessary to push the ingredients onto the blades.

Peel and core the apples. Fill the centre of the apples with the almond paste. Roll them in melted butter, then in crumbs and finally in the sugar. Place in a shallow, buttered baking dish and bake at 425°F/Reg 7 for 25 minutes or until tender. Serve with whipped cream.

Makes 4 servings.

Left, Cherry Pie, Nesselrode Chiffon Pie
Dessert Crêpes
Right, Regal Cheesecake, Lemon Crunch Pie
Almond Stuffed Apples

Regal Cheese Cake

1-ounce butter or margarine
6-ounce Marie biscuits
3-ounce castor sugar
2-ounce butter or margarine (softened)
3 eggs
1¼-pounds cream cheese (softened)
2 fluid ounce double cream
Yellow peel of ¼ lemon (thin strip)
Orange portion of peel of ¼ orange (thin
   strip)
6-ounce castor sugar
¼ teaspoon vanilla essence
1 egg yolk
3 tablespoons flour (plain)

Butter the sides and bottom of an 8 in. flan ring on a baking tray or a loose bottomed sandwich tin. Crumb the biscuits by dropping them through the hole in the lid onto the revolving blades until the blender will not crumb any more. Empty the goblet and start again. Repeat the process until all the biscuits are crumbed. Add 3-ounce sugar and 2-ounce butter and mix well. Press over the base and up the sides of the prepared tin. Blend 1 egg, ½ pound cream cheese, 1 fluid ounce cream, lemon and orange peel for 20 seconds. Scrape down the sides of the goblet with a spatula and blend for a further 30 seconds, adding 2-ounce sugar through the opening in the top of the lid whilst the motor is running. If necessary blend for a further 10 seconds having scraped down the sides of the goblet again. Empty into a large mixing bowl.

Blend 2 eggs, ½ pound cream cheese and vanilla essence for 20 seconds. Scrape down the sides of the goblet and blend for a further 30 seconds adding 2-ounce sugar through the hole in the lid whilst the motor is running. Add to the bowl. Blend the egg yolk, ¼ pound cream cheese, flour and remaining cream for 20 seconds, adding the last 2-ounce sugar through the hole in the lid whilst the motor is running. Add to the bowl and mix thoroughly.
Carefully spoon the cheese mixture into the prepared flan. Bake at 275°F/Reg 2 for 1 hour. Turn the oven off and leave the flan in the oven for 1 hour. Allow to cool very slowly at room temperature, then chill. Top with strawberry glaze; chill to set the glaze. Remove from the tin to serve.
Makes 6-8 servings.

Strawberry Glaze

Blend 2-ounce strawberries (washed and hulled), 2 fluid ounce water, 3-ounce castor sugar and 1½ teaspoons arrowroot for 5 seconds. Cook and stir until clear and thick. Add 4-ounce washed, hulled, sliced strawberries and spoon over the top of the cheese cake.

Lemon Crunch Pie

Ginger Crumb Crust

8-ounce ginger biscuits (crumbed in
   blender)
4-ounce butter or margarine (melted)

Filling

1 small tin condensed milk
Juice of 2 lemons
Rind of 1 lemon (grated)
¼ pint double cream

Add the gingernut crumbs to the melted fat and stir well. Press the mixture into either a lightly greased pie dish or a 7 in. fluted flan ring. Leave in a cool place or refrigerator to set.
Place all ingredients except the cream in the goblet and blend for 15 seconds. Remove centre cap and pour the cream in through the hole in the lid. Switch off as soon as the cream is incorporated. Place filling in the case and decorate with grated chocolate.
If a flan ring is used the crust must be very firm before the ring is removed.
Makes 6-8 servings.

Chocolate Dessert Pancakes

5-ounce plain flour
1 teaspoon baking powder
½ level teaspoon bicarbonate of soda
1 egg
1½-ounce castor sugar
1-ounce butter (softened)
4-ounce chocolate syrup
4-6 fluid ounce milk
2 drops of vanilla essence
2-ounce nuts
¼ pint double cream

Sieve the flour, baking powder and soda into a large bowl. Blend together egg, sugar, butter, chocolate syrup, 4 fluid ounce milk and vanilla essence. When smooth add the flour and nuts and reblend. If necessary use the spatula to push the mixture back onto the blades. The batter should be thick but spreadable.

If necessary add remaining 2 fluid ounce milk to make batter the correct consistency. Spoon into the base of a heavy based buttered frying pan. Bake on both sides. Serve with whipped cream.
Makes 2 dozen pancakes.

Dessert Crepes

Prepare in advance and freeze for that special event

8-10 almond macaroons
5-ounce plain flour
Pinch of salt
2 eggs
8 fluid ounce milk
2 level tablespoons castor sugar
1 tablespoon corn oil
3 tablespoons single cream

Make biscuit crumbs by feeding the macaroons onto the revolving blades of the blender. Empty out into small basin. Place the rest of the ingredients in the goblet and blend until smooth (45 seconds approx.). Let the batter stand for 10-20 minutes. Stir in the macaroon crumbs.

Heat a little butter in a frying pan and fry approx. 2 tablespoons of mixture at a time, turning to brown each side. Repeat with remaining batter. Stack the crêpes in a cloth to keep warm and moist.

Fill with desired fillings and then fold. Alternatively they can be rolled and an exciting sauce poured over.
Makes 6 servings.

Surprise Fudge Pudding

8-ounce plain flour
2½ level teaspoon baking powder
Pinch of salt
2-ounce butter or margarine (softened)
4-ounce castor sugar
6 fluid ounce milk
3-ounce walnuts or almonds
5-ounce soft brown sugar
1-ounce cocoa
8 fluid ounce boiling water

Sieve flour, baking powder and salt into a large mixing bowl. Blend together butter, sugar, milk and nuts for 30 seconds. Add to bowl with flour. Mix thoroughly and turn into a lightly buttered 2 pint pie dish.

Mix the brown sugar and cocoa together and sprinkle over the pudding mixture. Pour the boiling water over this. Bake at 375°F/Reg 5 for 40 minutes. Spoon into serving dishes so sauce is on top. Serve with cream.

Makes 6 servings.

Lemon Pudding

3 egg whites
1-ounce castor sugar
10 fluid ounce milk
5-ounce castor sugar
3 egg yolks
2-ounce butter or margarine (softened)
1 lemon (thinly pared peel and fruit
    only)
2-ounce plain flour

Whisk the egg whites until foamy. Gradually add 1-ounce sugar, and continue to beat until stiff. Place in the blender the milk, sugar, egg yolks, butter and lemon—blend for 30 seconds, adding flour through opening in top while motor is running. Pour over whites and fold in. Place in a 2 pint, lightly greased dish. Stand this in a meat tin containing water. Bake at 350°F/Reg 4 for 45-50 minutes.

This can be cooked in 8 small dishes at the same temperature but for 35-40 minutes.

Makes 4 servings.

Caramel Rice Pudding

8 fluid ounce milk
1 egg
5-ounce raisins
1-ounce brown sugar
Pinch of salt
2-ounce rice (short grain)
Cinnamon

Cook the rice in a little water until soft and drain. Blend all ingredients except rice and cinnamon together for 30 seconds. Mix with rice and cinnamon.

Place in a 1 pint lightly greased pudding dish. Set this in a baking tin of hot water. Bake at 350°F/ Reg 4 for 30 minutes.

Makes 4 servings.

Strawberry Torte

3-ounce Rich Tea biscuits
6 egg whites
2½-ounce castor sugar
6 egg yolks
5-ounce castor sugar
1 tablespoon brandy
4-ounce walnuts
1 teaspoon baking powder
Strawberry Bavarian Cream (see page 117)
Strawberries for decoration

Crumb the biscuits by dropping them through the hole in the lid onto the revolving blades. Place in bowl. Whisk egg whites with rotary beater until foamy, gradually add the 2½-ounce sugar—beat until stiff.

Place egg yolks, sugar and brandy in blender for 20 seconds adding nuts through the hole in the lid. Sprinkle baking powder over the crumbs. Fold the egg yolk mixture into the crumbs then carefully fold in the meringue. Spread carefully in 3 lightly greased, lined 8 in. sandwich tins. Bake at 350°F/Reg 4 for 15-20 minutes. Cool in tins for 5 minutes and then cool on racks. Spread the top of each layer with Strawberry Bavarian Cream. Stack layers. Decorate with strawberries.

Makes 6 servings.

Apricot Crème

1 large tin apricot halves
½ packet lemon jelly
1 envelope gelatine
2 (2 in.) pieces of lemon peel
½ tray of ice cubes
¼ pint double cream
Toasted coconut and mint sprigs for
  decoration

Drain the juice from the apricots. Heat 8 fluid
ounce of this to boiling. Allow to cool slightly
and then place in the goblet with apricot halves,
jelly, gelatine and lemon peel and blend for 10
seconds. Add the ice cubes and re-blend, adding
cream through opening in top while motor is
running. Pour into a 1-pint or 4 small moulds.
Chill until firm. Un-mould. Decorate with coconut
and sprigs of mint.
Makes 4 servings.

Apple Delight Pudding

6-ounce plain flour
1¼ teaspoons bicarbonate soda
1 teaspoon cinnamon
1 level teaspoon baking powder
Pinch of ground cloves
pinch of nutmeg
4 medium tart apples (cored and sliced)
1 egg
5-ounce castor sugar
2-ounce butter or margarine (softened)

Sieve together flour, soda, cinnamon, baking
powder and spices. Drop the apple slices onto the
revolving blades—tip this into the flour when the
goblet is approximately ¼ full and continue with
the rest. Blend egg, sugar and butter together
until smooth. Add to the flour and mix well.
Spread in lightly greased 8 in. square tin. Bake at
350°F/Reg 4 for 30 minutes. Serve with Butter
Sauce.
Makes 4 servings.

Butter Sauce

Heat 4-ounce butter, 5-ounce sugar and ¼ pint
double cream in saucepan until butter melts. Add
½ teaspoon vanilla essence and simmer for 30
minutes. Serve warm.

Rhubarb Cream Pie

½ pint hot water
5-ounce castor sugar
3 tablespoons cornflour
Pinch of salt
3 egg yolks
Thinly pared-off orange peel
10-ounce rhubarb (cut in 1 in. pieces)
½-ounce butter or margarine
1 (9 in.) unbaked pastry shell
3 egg whites
Pinch of cream of tartar
1½-ounce castor sugar

Blend water, sugar, cornflour and salt for 10 seconds. Empty into a saucepan, and bring to the boil. Simmer for 3 minutes stirring all the time. Place egg yolks, orange peel and hot cornflour mixture in the goblet and blend together for 15 seconds. Add the rhubarb and butter through opening in top, while motor is running.

Pour into pastry shell. Bake at 375° F/Reg 5 for 30-45 minutes, or until custard is set. Beat egg whites and cream of tartar with whisk until foamy. Add the 1½-ounce sugar and continue beating until stiff. Spread meringue over hot pie, carefully sealing to edges. Return to oven for 15-20 minutes or until meringue is golden. Cool before serving.

Makes 6 servings.

Steamed Date Pudding

2-ounce nuts
4-ounce dates (stoned)
10-ounce plain flour
1 rounded teaspoon bicarbonate of soda
1 rounded teaspoon baking powder
1½-ounce margarine
5-ounce castor sugar
1 egg
8 fluid ounce milk
¼ lemon (pared-off peel and fruit only)

Chop the nuts by dropping them onto the revolving blades through the hole in the lid. Chop the dates in the same way and empty into a bowl with nuts. Add the sieved flour, soda and baking powder to the same bowl.

Place margarine, sugar, egg, ½ the milk and lemon in the goblet and blend for 30 seconds. Add the other ½ milk and blend for a further 5 seconds. Add to the dry ingredients—mix well. Pour into a large well buttered basin and cover lightly with either a lid or foil. Steam for 2 hours checking the water level occasionally. Serve hot or cold with Lemon or Hard Sauce (*see* page 116).

Makes 6 servings.

Apricot Soufflé Pie

8-ounce dried apricots } together
2 fluid ounce water
3 eggs
7-ounce castor sugar
½ pint sour cream
1½ teaspoons vanilla essence
1 (9 in.) unbaked pastry shell

Soak the apricots in the water for approximately 1 hour. Blend the eggs for 10 seconds. Blend for a further 30 seconds, adding the sugar through the the hole in the lid whilst the motor is running. Add the apricots and water and blend for a further

20 seconds. Add the sour cream and vanilla essence. Blend for a final 10 seconds. Pour into the pastry shell or crumb crust, and bake at 375°F/Reg 5 for 45 minutes or until the filling is firm in the centre.

Makes 6 servings.

Cranberry Relish Pie

8-ounce shortcrust pastry (made up of
  8-ounce plain flour and 4-ounce fat)
1 tin of cranberries
4 small apples (cored)
1 medium orange (thin portion of peel
  and fruit only)
2-3-ounce walnuts
6-ounce castor sugar
2 tablespoons flour (plain)
½ teaspoon cinnamon
Salt to taste
¼ teaspoon nutmeg
½-ounce butter or margarine

Roll out half of the pastry and line a 9 in. plate or tin. Place the cranberries in the goblet and blend for 5 seconds. Pour into a bowl. Chop the apples by dropping them through the hole in the lid onto the revolving blades. When the blades are covered, empty and start the process again. Repeat the process until the apples are all chopped. Add them to the cranberries.

Chop the orange and nuts in the same manner and add to the cranberries and apples. Add the remaining ingredients except the pastry. Turn into the pastry shell and dot with butter. Roll out the remaining pastry and place over the pie. Seal the edges and flute, slashing the top. Bake at 425°F/Reg 7 for 30-40 minutes. Serve with Hard Sauce (*see* page 116).

Makes 6 servings.

Date Cream Pie

1 pint sour cream
2-ounce castor sugar
1½ level tablespoons cornflour
Salt to taste
2 eggs
6-ounce dates (stoned)
1-ounce walnuts
⅛ lemon (thin yellow portion of peel and
  fruit only)
1 (9 in.) baked pastry shell

Blend half of the sour cream, castor sugar, cornflour and salt for 10 seconds. Pour into a saucepan and cook, stirring constantly over a low heat until slightly thickened. Blend the remaining sour cream, eggs, dates, walnuts, lemon peel and fruit for 20 seconds. Add to sour cream mixture in the saucepan and stir. Cook and stir over a low heat until thick—about 3 minutes. Turn into pastry shell and chill.

Makes 6 servings.

Dutch Apple Pie

1½-pounds apples (peeled and sliced)
1 (9 in.) unbaked pastry shell
7-ounce castor sugar
¼ pint cream
1 egg
2 tablespoons flour (plain)
2 teaspoons cinnamon
2-ounce walnuts
½-ounce butter or margarine
1 teaspoon vanilla essence
4-ounce Cheddar cheese (cubed)

Arrange the apples in the pastry shell. Blend the sugar, cream, egg, flour and cinnamon for 30 seconds. Add nuts, butter and vanilla and blend for a further 5 seconds. Pour over the apples. Bake at 350°F/Reg 4 for 45-50 minutes or until the apples are tender.

Grate the cheese in the blender. Sprinkle over the hot pie and leave to cool slightly before serving.

Makes 6 servings.

Mocha Bavarian Cream

Mocha Bavarian Cream

¼ pint hot strong coffee
2 fluid ounce cold water
1 packet gelatine
6-ounce plain chocolate (cubed)
1 tablespoon sugar
2 egg yolks
½ tray of ice cubes
¼ pint double cream

Blend together coffee, water and gelatine for 10 seconds. Add chocolate, sugar and eggs, re-blend for 10 seconds. Ice and cream should be added through the hole in the lid whilst the motor is running. Pour into a 1 pint mould and chill. Serve with Mocha Sauce (*see* page 76).
Makes 4 servings.

Lemon Angel Pie

You can fill the delicate Angel Pie with fresh or frozen fruit, prepared whipped dessert mix or prepared pudding or pie filling

Angel Pie shell (*see* page 112)
4 egg yolks
3-ounce castor sugar
1 lemon (thin yellow portion peel only)
½ lemon (peeled)
1 teaspoon vanilla essence
3 tablespoons sugar
½ pint double cream (whipped)

Prepare the Angel Pie shell as in Chocolate Angel Pie (*see* page 112). Blend egg yolks, sugar, lemon peel and fruit for 30 seconds. Pour into a saucepan and cook, stirring over a low heat until it has thickened. Cool, stirring occasionally. Add vanilla and sugar to the whipped cream and spread half of the cream over the bottom of the cooled Angel Pie shell. Top with lemon filling and then with the remaining cream, allowing lemon filling to show around the edges and centre. Chill for 2-3 hours.
Makes 6-8 servings.

Cottage Cheese Pie

A rich fruited custard pie

8-ounce dried apricots or stoned prunes
  (soaked overnight)
4-ounce cottage cheese
2 eggs
5-ounce castor sugar
Salt to taste
¼ pint milk
¼ pint double cream
1 (9 in.) baked pastry shell

Chop the apricots for 15 seconds by dropping them through the hole in the lid onto the revolving blades, and spread over the bottom of the pastry shell. Blend the cottage cheese, eggs, sugar and salt for 20 seconds. Add the milk and cream and blend for 10 seconds. Pour over the apricots. Bake at 450°F/Reg 8 for 10 minutes, lower the heat to 325°F/Reg 3 and bake for 1 hour or until a knife inserted into the centre comes out clean.
Makes 6 servings.

Creamy Chocolate Pie

½ pint double cream
½ pint milk (hot)
8-ounce marshmallows
2-ounce plain chocolate (broken into
  squares)
1 teaspoon vanilla essence
Salt to taste
2-ounce walnuts
1 (9 in.) baked pastry shell
1-ounce coconut

Whip the cream in the blender until it reaches piping consistency. Empty this into a bowl and chill. Blend the milk, marshmallows, chocolate, vanilla essence and salt for 60 seconds. Chill in the container until the mixture mounds when spooned. Add the walnuts and chop for 10 seconds. Pour over the whipped cream—fold together. Turn into a pastry shell; top with coconut. Chill until firm.
Makes 6 servings.

Ginger Special

½-pound ginger biscuits (halved)
4-ounce butter or margarine (melted)
½ pint milk (scalded)
2 egg yolks
2-ounce castor sugar
3 teaspoons cornflour
1-ounce plain chocolate
1 teaspoon vanilla essence
1 packet gelatine
2-ounce cold water
1 tablespoon cognac
2 egg whites
3-ounce castor sugar
¼ pint double cream
Grated chocolate for decoration

Crumb the ginger biscuits by dropping the halved biscuits through the hole in the lid onto the revolving blades until the blender stops crumbing them. Empty the crumbs into a bowl and start the process again until all the biscuits have been crumbed. Add the butter and mix well. Press over the bottom and up the sides of a 7-8 in. flan ring. Put aside to set in a cool place. Blend the milk, egg yolks, sugar and cornflour for 20 seconds. Pour into the saucepan and cook, stirring all the time over a medium heat until the mixture coats a wooden spoon.

Pour half of the hot custard mixture into the blender goblet and add the chocolate along with the vanilla essence. Blend for 30 seconds, stopping the motor to push the ingredients onto the blades. Blend for 30 seconds longer, if necessary, to melt all the chocolate. Pour the chocolate mixture into the crust and chill. Wash the goblet and blend the remaining custard, gelatine and water for 30 seconds. Add the cognac and blend for 20 seconds longer. Whisk the egg whites until foamy. Gradually add the sugar and beat until stiff. Pour the custard over the egg whites and fold until smooth. Pour over the chocolate layer in the pastry shell and chill. Spread the whipped cream over the top and sprinkle with grated chocolate.
Makes 5-6 servings.

Baked Caramel Custard

3-ounce castor sugar
1 pint milk (hot)
4 eggs
1 teaspoon vanilla essence

Melt the sugar in a small heavy based pan over medium heat until it forms an amber-coloured syrup. Place hot milk, eggs, vanilla and salt in the goblet and blend for 10 seconds, adding syrup and sugar through opening in top while the motor is running.

Pour into shallow pie dish and stand this in a meat tin holding hot water. Bake at 350° F/Reg 4 for 45-50 minutes or until knife inserted in centre comes out clean. Serve hot or cold.
Makes 4 servings.

Pineapple Cream

4 fluid ounce hot pineapple juice
2 envelopes gelatine
½ lemon (peel and pith removed)
2 fluid ounce maraschino cherry juice
1½-ounce castor sugar
3 fluid ounce double cream
12 maraschino cherries
1 tray of ice cubes

Place pineapple juice, gelatine, lemon and maraschino juice in the blender and run for 45 seconds. Add sugar, cream and cherries and blend for 5 seconds. Add ice and allow to run until the mixture is smooth. Leave to stand for 1 minute. Spoon into serving dishes.

A 10-ounce packet of frozen raspberries, partially thawed can be used instead of cherries and juice.
Makes 4 servings.

Cherry Jubilee Pie

1 tin cherry pie filling
1 unbaked pastry shell (8 in.)
8-ounce cream cheese (cubed)
1 egg
3-ounce castor sugar
1 teaspoon vanilla essence
$\frac{1}{4}$ pint sour cream

Pour the pie filling into the pastry shell and bake at 425°F/Reg 7 for 15 minutes. Blend the cream cheese, egg, sugar and vanilla essence for 30 seconds. Scrape down the sides of the blender if necessary and blend for a further 30 seconds, or until smooth. Pour over the cherry pie and spread evenly. Bake at 350°F/Reg 4 for 30 minutes. Cool on a rack. Spread sour cream over the top and sprinkle with nutmeg. Chill.
Makes 6-8 servings.

Raisin Pie

4-ounce prunes (stoned) ⎫ soaked
2 fluid ounce warm water ⎬ together
                         ⎭ for 1 hour
2-ounce walnuts
3 eggs
6 fluid ounce honey
$\frac{1}{4}$ lemon (thin yellow portion of peel
   and fruit only)
4-ounce raisins
$\frac{1}{2}$ pint sour cream
1 (9 in.) unbaked pastry shell

Chop the nuts by dropping them through the hole in the lid onto the revolving blades—empty into bowl. Blend the eggs, honey and lemon for 10 seconds. Add the prunes and raisins and chop for 10 seconds. Scrape down the sides of the goblet and blend for a further 10 seconds. Add the sour cream and blend for a final 20 seconds. Pour into the pastry shell, and sprinkle with nuts. Bake at 350°F/Reg 4 for 50-60 minutes.
Makes 6 servings.

Apricot Custard

$\frac{3}{4}$ pint milk
4-ounce dried apricots
$1\frac{1}{2}$-ounce castor sugar
3 eggs
Pinch of salt

Blend all the ingredients in the goblet for 45 seconds. Pour the custard into 6 lightly buttered individual moulds.
Place these in a meat tin containing hot water. Bake at 350°F/Reg 4 for 45 minutes or until a knife inserted in centre comes out clean.
Makes 4 servings.

Baked Prune Whip

2 egg whites
1-ounce castor sugar
2-ounce nuts
$\frac{1}{2}$-pound prunes (stoned)
8 fluid ounce water
$\frac{1}{2}$ lemon (pared-off peel and fruit only)
$\frac{1}{2}$ level teaspoon cinnamon
3-ounce castor sugar
4 egg yolks
2 fluid ounce water (cold)
2 tablespoons cornflour
Pinch of salt
4 fluid ounce hot water

Beat the egg whites until foamy, gradually adding 1-ounce sugar—beat until stiff. Chop the nuts and empty onto a piece of paper. Blend together prunes, 8 fluid ounce water, lemon peel, fruit and cinnamon for 20 seconds. Add to egg whites. Place sugar, egg yolks, 2 fluid ounce cold water, cornflour and salt in blender and run for 10 seconds. Add hot water and blend for further 30 seconds. Add to egg whites.
Fold all ingredients together. Pour into a large shallow baking dish. Sprinkle nuts over. Bake at 350°F/Reg 4 for 40 minutes. Serve with Vanilla Sauce (*see* page 116).
Makes 4 servings.

Lemon Chiffon Pie

4 egg yolks
3-ounce castor sugar
1 packet gelatine
½ lemon (thin yellow portion of the peel
   and fruit only)
2 fluid ounce water
Salt to taste
4 egg whites
3-ounce castor sugar
1 (9 in.) baked pastry shell or crumb
   crust

Blend the egg yolks, 3-ounce sugar, gelatine, lemon, water and salt for 40 seconds. Pour into a saucepan and cook, stirring over a low heat until slightly thickened. Chill until beginning to set. Beat the egg whites until foamy. Gradually add the sugar and beat to stiff peaks. Pour the egg yolk mixture over the egg whites and fold until smooth. Turn into the pastry shell and chill until firm.

Makes 6 servings.

Lemon Light Cheesecake

1 envelope gelatine
¼ lemon (pared-off peel and fruit only)
4 fluid ounce hot milk
1-ounce castor sugar
2 egg yolks
1 (8-ounce) packed cream cheese (cubed)
4 fluid ounce double cream
½ tray of ice cubes
4-ounce digestive biscuits (crumbed)

Place gelatine, lemon peel, fruit and hot milk in the goblet and blend for 30 seconds. Add sugar, egg yolks and cream cheese and continue to blend until smooth, adding cream and ice through opening in top while motor is running.
Pour into one large or 6 small dishes. Liberally sprinkle with biscuit crumbs. Chill until firm.
Makes 4 servings.

With the advent of machinery in the kitchen all the hard work has been taken out of bread-making. Our Yeast Rolls recipe is a good basic one and the three special breads we have given—Date Corn Bread, Orange Nut Bread and Golden Cheese Bread—are simply delicious. For special occasions the Peach Chiffon Party Cake is a dream.

With the use of your blender many recipes that appear to be difficult can be tackled with confidence by novice cooks. Torte Elegant that looks most sophisticated is simple and satisfying to make with the blender.

Bread and Cakes

1 Torte
2 Torte Elegant
3 Hot Milk Sponge
4 Banbury Tarts
5 Peach Chiffon Party Cake

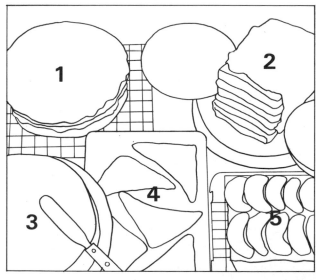

Torte

6-ounce digestive biscuits
4-ounce nuts
2 rounded tablespoons plain flour
2 teaspoons baking powder
4-ounce margarine or butter
5-ounce castor sugar
3 eggs
6 fluid ounce milk
Pinch of salt

Decoration

$\frac{1}{4}$ pint double cream (whipped)
Crystallised ginger

Crumb the digestive biscuits by dropping them onto the revolving blades. Place the crumbs in a large bowl. Chop the nuts in the same way and add to the crumbs. Add flour, baking powder and salt, mix thoroughly. Place the butter, sugar, eggs and milk in the goblet and blend for 30 seconds.

Add to dry ingredients and stir until moistened. Pour into 2 lightly greased 8 in. sandwich tins. Bake at 350°F/Reg 4 for 25-30 minutes. Cool for 10 minutes in the tin and then turn onto a cooling rack. Fill with whipped cream. Decorate with ginger.

Banbury Tarts

Make up 6-ounce shortcrust pastry
3 plain biscuits (e.g. Rich Tea)
2-ounce raisins
$\frac{1}{2}$ lemon (thin yellow portion of peel and fruit only)
2-ounce walnuts
1 egg yolk
3-ounce castor sugar
$\frac{1}{2}$-ounce butter or margarine

Roll the pastry into an 8 × 8 in. square. Cut into four 4-in. squares. Crumb the biscuits in the blender. Place in a bowl. Turn the blender on and drop the lemon, walnuts, raisins through the hole in the lid onto the revolving blades. Add egg yolk, sugar and buttter and blend for a further 10 seconds. Add to the biscuit crumbs and mix thoroughly. Spread over half of each pastry square. Moisten the edges, fold in triangles and seal. Prick the tops. Bake on a baking tray at 425°F/Reg 7 for 12-15 minutes.
Makes 4 tarts.

Peach Chiffon Party Cake

4 egg whites
$\frac{1}{4}$ teaspoon cream of tartar
1-ounce castor sugar
2-ounce walnuts (chopped in blender)
5-ounce plain flour
1$\frac{1}{2}$ teaspoons baking powder
Pinch of salt
3 egg yolks
6 tablespoons water
2 fluid ounce corn oil
2-ounce soft brown sugar
$\frac{1}{2}$ teaspoon vanilla essence
$\frac{1}{2}$ teaspoon almond essence
1 large tin sliced peaches (drained)
$\frac{1}{4}$ pint double cream (whipped)

Beat egg whites and cream of tartar with whisk until foamy. Gradually add 1 ounce sugar continuing to beat until the mixture is stiff. Stir the chopped nuts into the meringue mixture. Sieve flour, baking powder and salt into a large bowl. Place egg yolks, water, oil, brown sugar and essence in the goblet and blend for 20 seconds. Add this mixture to the flour and stir until thoroughly mixed. Pour this onto the meringue mixture and stir gently till all ingredients are thoroughly mixed. Turn into a lined greased Swiss roll tin. Bake at 375°F/Reg 5 for 15-20 minutes. Turn onto cooling rack and remove paper.

When cool cut the cake in half to form 2 rectangles. Place half of the peaches in the goblet and blend until smooth. Add half the cream and spread the mixture on one piece of cake, topping it with the other piece. Spread the rest of the whipped cream on the top and decorate with the rest of the fruit. Refrigerate before serving.

Hot Milk Sponge

6-ounce self-raising flour
1½ teaspoons baking powder
Salt to taste
2 eggs
5-ounce castor sugar
1 teaspoon vanilla essence
4 fluid ounce milk (scalded)
1-ounce butter or margarine

Sieve baking powder, flour and salt into a bowl. Blend the eggs for 20 seconds. Add sugar and vanilla and blend for a further 30 seconds. Add the flour mixture and blend for a further 20 seconds. Empty into bowl and add the milk and butter which have been previously combined. Stir only until mixed. Pour into two 7 in. tins which have been lined and greased. Bake at 350°F/Reg 4 for 25-30 minutes.

Chocolate Cream Cake

Sandwich the cakes together with the filling from the Chocolate Angel Pie recipe (*see* page 112).

Chocolate Icing

4 tablespoons hot milk
1-ounce butter or margarine (softened)
2-ounce plain chocolate (broken into
   squares)
½ teaspoon vanilla essence
12-ounce icing sugar
3-ounce cream cheese (optional)

Blend the milk, butter, chocolate and vanilla together for 30 seconds. Gradually add the sieved sugar through the hole in the lid until a spreading consistency is achieved. More milk can be added if necessary. Finally, feed the cubed cheese in through the top.

Torte Elegant

3 eggs
6-ounce castor sugar
¼ pint hot milk
1-ounce butter or margarine
8-ounce self-raising flour
1¼ teaspoons baking powder
Salt to taste
½ teaspoon vanilla essence

Blend eggs, sugar, hot milk and butter for 10 seconds. Sieve together the flour, baking powder and salt. Blend for 30 seconds adding the flour through the hole in the lid while the motor is running. Add vanilla essence and scrape down the sides of the goblet with a spatula. Blend for a further 10 seconds. Spread evenly in a large lined Swiss roll tin. Bake at 375°F/Reg 5 for 10-12 minutes. Cool slightly. Turn onto a cooling rack and remove the paper. Cut into quarters. Frost each section with White Cake Icing (*see* page 142). Stack layers and frost the sides of the torte. Decorate with grated chocolate if you wish. Chill.

You may turn the baked cake out onto a towel covered with castor sugar, remove paper and roll up as for a Swiss roll. Cool, then unroll, fill and reroll. Chill.

135

Yeast Rolls

¼-ounce dried or ½-ounce fresh yeast
8 fluid ounce warm milk and water
  mixed
1-ounce butter
1 level tablespoon sugar
1 teaspoon salt
1 egg
1-pound strong flour

Blend the yeast and warm liquid together for 5 seconds. Add the butter, sugar, salt and egg and blend for a further 15 seconds. Add 6 ounce of flour and blend for 20 seconds. Pour into large mixing bowl. Add remaining flour to make a soft dough. Turn onto a lightly floured surface and knead until dough is smooth and elastic. Return to the bowl, cover and leave to rise in a warm place until double its size. If plain buns are required then shape as desired.

Place rolls on greased baking sheet and leave in a warm place to prove (10-15 minutes). Bake at 425° F/Reg 7 for 15-20 minutes.

Cinnamon Rolls

After it has risen divide the basic yeast dough in half. On a lightly floured surface roll each half into 8 × 18 in. rectangle. Chop 2 ounce walnuts by dropping them through the hole in the lid onto the revolving blades. Switch the blender off and add 4-ounce brown sugar, 2-ounce melted butter and 1½ teaspoons cinnamon and blend for 20 seconds. Spread half the mixture onto each rectangle. Roll fairly tightly lengthwise. Cut into 1½ in. slices and place cut side up in two 8 in. square tins. Brush with melted butter. Cover and let prove in a warm place for 15 minutes. Bake at 400° F/Reg 6 for 20-25 minutes.

Cheese Rolls

Prepare and bake in the same way as for Cinnamon Rolls using 4-ounce grated cheese on each 8 × 18 in. rectangle.

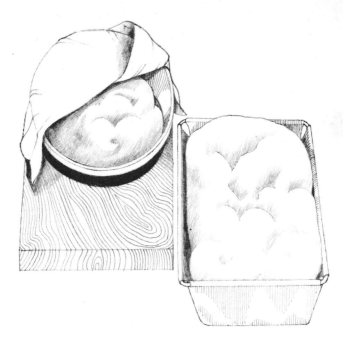

Golden Cheese Bread

1-pound strong flour
8 fluid ounce milk (scalded)
2 teaspoons sugar
1-ounce butter or margarine
Salt to taste
2 fluid ounce warm water
¼-ounce dried yeast or ½-ounce fresh
  yeast
1 egg
4-ounce Cheddar cheese (cubed)
½ tablespoon poppy seed

Sieve flour into a large bowl. Combine milk, sugar, butter and salt. Cool to lukewarm. Blend the water and yeast for 5 seconds. Add the egg and milk mixture and blend for 30 seconds, adding the cheese through the opening in the top whilst the motor is running. Pour over the flour and mix well. Turn onto a floured surface and knead well for 10 minutes adding more flour if necessary.

Replace in the bowl and brush the surface with oil before allowing to rise in a warm place until it has doubled in bulk. Knock the dough back by re-kneading. Place the dough into a 2 pound loaf tin and brush with melted butter. Sprinkle with poppy seed, and cover before leaving to prove (20-25 minutes).

Bake at 425° F/Reg 7 until it is light brown and sounds hollow underneath. Cool on rack.

Applesauce Cake

10-ounce plain flour
1½ teaspoons baking powder
Pinch of salt
½ teaspoon bicarbonate of soda
1 teaspoon cinnamon
½ teaspoon ground cloves
½ teaspoon nutmeg
½ teaspoon mixed spice
2 eggs
7-ounce castor sugar
8 fluid ounce apple sauce
3-ounce margarine
½ lemon (pared-off peel and fruit only)
2 tablespoons cocoa
2-ounce raisins
1-ounce walnuts

Sieve the flour, baking powder, salt, soda and spices into a large bowl. Blend together the eggs, sugar, apple sauce, butter, lemon and cocoa until smooth. Add raisins and walnuts and re-blend for 10 seconds.
Pour into bowl with dry ingredients and mix thoroughly. Cook in a lined 9 in. square cake tin at 350°F/Reg 4 for 80-85 minutes. Frost before serving.

Chocolate Cake

11-ounce self-raising flour
4 teaspoons baking powder
Salt to taste
4 fluid ounce milk
2-ounce plain chocolate (cubed)
2 eggs
8 fluid ounce milk
11-ounce castor sugar
3-ounce butter or margarine
1 teaspoon vanilla essence

Sieve together the flour, baking powder and salt into a bowl. Heat the 4 fluid ounce milk to luke-warm; add the chocolate. Blend the eggs, 8 fluid ounce milk, sugar, fat, warm milk and chocolate and vanilla for 30 seconds. Scrape down the sides of the goblet and blend for a further 30 seconds. Pour the blend in the goblet over the flour mixture

and beat until thoroughly mixed. Pour into 2 greased, lined, floured, deep 8 in. sandwich tins. Bake at 375°F/Reg 5 for 30 minutes. Cool in the tins for 10 minutes. Turn out onto racks and cool completely. Frost with frosting of your own choice.

Yellow Cake

12-ounce plain flour
4 teaspoons baking powder
½ teaspoon salt
2-ounce butter (softened)
7-ounce castor sugar
2 eggs
1 teaspoon vanilla essence
8 fluid ounce milk

Sieve flour, baking powder, salt into a large bowl. Blend butter, sugar, eggs, vanilla essence and milk until smooth. Add to flour and stir in very thoroughly. Pour into two 8 in. greased sandwich tins. Bake at 375°F/Reg 5 for 30 minutes.
Frost with French Butter Cream before serving.

Nut Cake

Add 2 ounce chopped nuts to flour.

Butter Chews

4-ounce almonds or walnuts
8-ounce plain flour (sieved)
1½-ounce castor sugar
4-ounce butter or margarine
3 egg whites
1½-ounce brown sugar
3 egg yolks
9-ounce brown sugar
3-ounce coconut

Chop the nuts in the blender by dropping them through the hole in the lid. Empty out and put to one side.

Place the flour and sugar in a large bowl and rub the margarine in until it resembles coarse breadcrumbs. Pack into the bottom of a well greased small Swiss roll tin and bake at 375°F/Reg 5 for 15 minutes.

Beat the egg whites until foamy. Gradually add the 1½-ounce brown sugar and continue beating until stiff.

Place egg yolks and 9-ounce sugar in the goblet and blend for 10-15 seconds. Pour into a bowl with egg whites, add the nuts and coconut. Fold in gently until smooth. Pour over baked layer and spread evenly. Continue to bake at 375°F/Reg 5 for further 25-30 minutes. Cool and cut into squares.

Date Nut Roll

3-ounce digestive biscuits
2-ounce nuts
½-pound dates (stoned)
3 fluid ounce double cream
½-pound marshmallows (cut into quarters)

¼ pint double cream
Maraschino cherries

Crumb the digestive biscuits by dropping onto the revolving blades of the blender. Put 2-ounce of crumbs in a bowl and reserve the other ounce. Chop the nuts and dates in the blender by feeding through the hole in the lid with the motor run-ning. Combine these with the 2-ounce crumbs. Stir in the cream and then add the marshmallows. Shape into a roll on greaseproof or waxed paper. Roll in the 1-ounce of crumbs. Chill for several hours. Slice and serve. Top each with whipped cream and a maraschino cherry.

This can be served up as a teatime cookie if sliced and the decoration omitted.

Rich Apricot Fingers

5-ounce dried apricots
2 fluid ounce warm water
4-ounce plain flour (sieved)
2-ounce butter or margarine (softened)
1-ounce granulated sugar
1½-ounce self-raising flour (sieved)
Pinch of salt
2-ounce walnuts
6-ounce soft brown sugar
½ teaspoon vanilla essence
2 eggs

Blend the apricots and warm water together for 15 seconds, then set aside. Rub the 2-ounce butter into the plain flour, stir in the granulated sugar and pack this tightly into the bottom of a greased 8 in. square tin. Bake at 325°F/Reg 3 for 25 minutes. Place the flour (self-raising) in the bowl. Chop the nuts in the blender by dropping them through the hole in the lid. Switch off and add the brown sugar, vanilla, apricots and eggs; blend for a further 20 seconds.

Pour into the bowl with the flour and mix thor-oughly. Spread over baked layer and bake a further 25 minutes at 325°F/Reg 3. Cool and sprinkle with icing sugar. Cut into 16 fingers.

Orange Spice Cake

10-ounce plain flour
1½ level teaspoons baking powder
1 level teaspoon cinnamon
Pinch of salt
½ level teaspoon ground cloves
½ level teaspoon nutmeg
4-ounce raisins
8 fluid ounce water
5-ounce castor sugar
4-ounce margarine (softened)
1 egg
2-ounce walnuts
1 small orange (pared-off peel and fruit
  only)
2½-ounce castor sugar

Sieve together flour, baking powder, cinnamon, salt, cloves and nutmeg. Place raisins, water, sugar, margarine and egg in the goblet and blend for 20-30 seconds. Pour into the bowl with the dry ingredients and mix well. Pour into a lightly greased 9 in. square tin and bake at 350° F/Reg 4 for 40-45 minutes.
Blend together the orange peel, fruit and sugar for 20 seconds. Pour over cake as soon as it comes from oven. Cool cake in tin.

Mexican Wedding Cakes

4-ounce walnuts or almonds
10-ounce plain flour (sieved)
Pinch of salt
4-ounce butter or margarine (softened)
2-ounce castor sugar
1 teaspoon vanilla essence

Chop the nuts by feeding on to the revolving blades. Empty nuts into mixing bowl—add flour and salt.
Place butter, sugar and vanilla essence in goblet —blend for 30 seconds. Scrape mixture from side of goblet and blend for a further 30 seconds. Place this mixture in bowl with nuts and flour—mix well.
Place in teaspoonfuls on lightly greased sheet.

Bake at 325° F/Reg 3 for 20 minutes. When cool roll the balls lightly in icing sugar. Store in an airtight jar.

Banana Chiffon Cake

7-ounce self-raising flour
Salt to taste
2 teaspoons baking powder
4 egg whites
¼ teaspoon cream of tartar
1 medium banana (peeled)
3 egg yolks
3 fluid ounce cold water
2 fluid ounce salad oil
6 ounce castor sugar
½ teaspoon vanilla essence

Sieve together the flour, salt and baking powder. Beat the egg whites and cream of tartar until it forms soft peaks. Chop the banana in the blender by dropping it through the hole in the lid of the goblet onto the revolving blades. Add the egg yolks, water, oil, sugar and vanilla and blend for 30 seconds. Scrape down the sides of the blender and blend for a further 10 seconds. Pour into the bowl with the flour and stir until smooth. Fold the flour mixture into the egg whites. Turn into two 8 in. greased, lined, floured tins and bake at 325° F/Reg 3 for 30 minutes or until the cake feels firm in the middle. Remove from tins onto a cooling rack and cool. Cover with icing or frosting of your choice.

Orange Nut Bread, Cinnamon Bun and Date Corn Bread

Orange Nut Bread

1-pound plain flour
$\frac{1}{4}$ teaspoon bicarbonate soda
$2\frac{1}{2}$ teaspoons baking powder
Salt to taste
2-ounce walnuts
Peel of 1 orange (thin orange coloured
    portion only)
Fruit of 1 orange
6 fluid ounce milk
3-ounce light brown sugar
3 tablespoons black treacle
1-ounce butter or margarine (softened)

Sieve flour, soda, baking powder and salt—set aside. Chop the walnuts by dropping them through the hole in the lid onto the revolving blades and then add them to the flour. Blend the orange peel, fruit, milk, sugar, treacle and butter for 30 seconds. Add to the flour and mix well. Pour into a paper-lined 2 pound loaf tin. Bake at 350°F/Reg 4 for 1 hour or until a skewer inserted into the middle comes out clean. Remove from the tin and cool completely before slicing.

Date Corn Bread

6-ounce plain flour
2 teaspoons baking powder
Salt to taste
6 fluid ounce milk
1 egg
2 tablespoons corn oil
3 tablespoons sugar
10 dates (stoned)

Sieve together the flour, baking powder and salt. Blend the egg, milk, corn oil and sugar for 10 seconds. Add the dates through the hole in the lid whilst the motor is still running. Add the sieved dry ingredients and blend for 10 seconds. Pour into a greased 2 pound tin and bake at 400°F/Reg 6 for 20-25 minutes.

Top, Butter Chews
Centre, Date Nut Roll
Bottom, Rich Apricot Fingers

Frosting

4 almond macaroons
1-ounce walnuts
2-ounce maraschino cherries
10-ounce castor sugar
4 fluid ounce water
1 tablespoon golden syrup
2 egg whites
1 teaspoon vanilla essence
Whole drained maraschino cherries
Walnut halves

Prepare crumbs from the macaroons by dropping through the hole in the lid. Empty into the bowl. Chop the walnuts and cherries in the same way and empty into the same bowl. Place sugar, water and syrup in a saucepan, bring to the boil and simmer for 3-4 minutes to soft ball stage.

Beat egg whites until stiff, pour syrup over in fine stream whilst continuing to beat. The frosting should stand in stiff peaks when ready. Add vanilla. Fold ⅓ of the frosting into macaroon crumbs, walnuts and maraschino cherries—use this as the filling for a cake. Spread the remaining frosting over top and sides of cake. Decorate with whole cherries and walnut halves.

Whipped Cream Frosting

Especially good on chocolate cake

½ pint double cream
½ packet gelatine
2 tablespoons cold water
¼ lemon (thin portion of the yellow peel and fruit only)
2 tablespoons icing sugar (sieved)
Salt to taste

Reserve 2 tablespoons double cream and whisk the remainder as directed on page 117. Scald 2 tablespoons of cream and blend with the gelatine and water for 40 seconds. Add lemon, sugar and salt and blend for a further 20 seconds. Pour into a bowl and chill until it reaches the consistency of unbeaten egg white. Fold the chilled gelatine into the whipped cream until smooth.

Makes enough frosting to fill and frost 2 (8 or 9 in.) round layers. Chill the frosted cake until serving.

White Cake Icing

1 egg
1½-ounce butter or margarine (softened)
1 tablespoon milk
1 teaspoon vanilla essence
14-ounce icing sugar (sieved)

Blend together the egg, milk, vanilla essence and 4-ounce icing sugar. Empty into a mixing bowl. Gradually add remaining sugar and mix by hand until of spreading consistency.

For orange or lemon icing, substitute orange or lemon juice for milk.

French Butter Cream

6-ounce peppermint flavoured chocolate
   (broken into squares)
2 fluid ounce boiling water or hot
   strong coffee
4 egg yolks
2-ounce butter or margarine (softened)
1-ounce icing sugar (sieved)
½ teaspoon vanilla essence

Blend chocolate and water or coffee for 20 seconds. Add egg yolks, butter, sugar and vanilla and blend for a further 20 seconds.

Chill frosting if necessary, until of spreading consistency.

Index